D1084367

DIVIDED POLITICS, DIVIDED NATION

DIVIDED POLITICS,

DIVIDED NATION

HYPERCONFLICT
in the TRUMP ERA

DARRELL M. WEST

BROOKINGS INSTITUTION PRESS
Washington, D.C.

The Brookings Institution is a private nonprofit organization devoted to research, education, and publication on important issues of domestic and foreign policy. Its principal purpose is to bring the highest quality independent research and analysis to bear on current and emerging policy problems. Interpretations or conclusions in Brookings publications should be understood to be solely those of the authors.

Library of Congress Cataloging-in-Publication Data

Names: West, Darrell M., 1954– author.
Title: Divided politics, divided nation : hyperconflict in the Trump era / by
    Darrell M. West.
Description: Washington, D.C. : Brookings Institution Press, 2019. |
    Includes bibliographical references and index.
Identifiers: LCCN 2019001457 (print) | LCCN 2019002324 (ebook) |
    ISBN 9780815736929 (ebook) | ISBN 9780815736912 (hardcover : alk.
    paper)
Subjects: LCSH: Political culture—United States. | Polarization (Social
    sciences)—Political aspects—United States. | Trump, Donald, 1946– |
    United States—Politics and government—2017– | United States—
    Politics and government—Public opinion.
Classification: LCC JK1726 (ebook) | LCC JK1726 .W4 2019 (print) |
    DDC 973.933—dc23
LC record available at https://lccn.loc.gov/2019001457

9 8 7 6 5 4 3 2 1

Typeset in Goudy Oldstyle

Composition by Elliott Beard

To Ken, Joanne, and Shirley
United we stand, divided we fall.

CONTENTS

Contents

Contents

DIVIDED POLITICS, DIVIDED NATION

UPHEAVAL

I watched the 2016 election returns in stunned silence. Along with nearly every other political expert, I thought Democrat Hillary Clinton would coast to victory over Republican Donald Trump. I had heard her speak at the Brookings Institution in Washington, D.C., where I worked, and been impressed with her in-depth knowledge about a wide range of issues.

This was in stark contrast to her GOP opponent, who came across as rash and impulsive during the campaign, and not very informed. He had started his quixotic quest for the presidency by condemning Mexican immigrants and calling for an America First policy that repudiated decades of U.S. global engagement.

Four years earlier, I had seen his combative nature up close. In 2012, when Republicans were considering him for a prime-time speaking role at their national convention, I had taken a playful jab at him in a media commentary. "Republicans should send Trump on an all-expenses-paid trip around the world at the time of their convention," I joked. If the party gives him a prominent platform, "he brings nothing but trouble to the GOP."[1]

1

The morning this quote appeared in *Politico*, I received a call from Lauren Kelly, Trump's executive assistant. She asked for my e-mail address, which I gave to her. Shortly thereafter, I received an e-mail in which the billionaire had pasted my quote into the message and written in big, black, bold letters "Darrell, you are a 'fool.' Best wishes, Donald J. Trump." I was stunned the celebrity cared what an academic said about him.

Two years later, I published a book called *Billionaires* that detailed the political clout of the ultrawealthy.[2] As part of its promotion, Brookings had published a list of top billionaires who had been influential in the midterm election. Since he had few campaign contributions and little political activity, I had rated Trump eighteenth on the list, well below billionaires such as Charles and David Koch, Michael Bloomberg, and Bill Gates.[3]

Sitting at my desk one day, the phone rang with the caller ID of Trump Org. The caller was not Trump but his bulldog lawyer, Michael Cohen, the "fixer" who paid porn star Stormy Daniels $130,000 during the campaign to keep quiet about her affair with Trump.[4] The attorney wanted to know why the billionaire was rated so low when he clearly deserved to be near the top. He said that Trump had taped a number of influential "robo-calls" on behalf of conservative candidates, and most of the aspirants had won. Would I consider revising the ranking and moving Trump up the list, Cohen inquired.[5]

My answer to the attorney was in the negative, but after witnessing Trump's thin skin and erratic performance during the campaign, I was dumbfounded in 2016 when he won the top office. Speaking to ordinary folks across the country who had not shared in economic prosperity, Trump told them they had been betrayed by coastal elites who had pushed bad trade deals and flawed economic programs. Experts—of the sort I worked with at Brookings—had sold them down the river, he said, and it was necessary to take decisive action that would disrupt the status quo and "make America great again." According to Trump, it was time to enact fundamental changes and restore the country to its preeminent position of an earlier era, when

America was not undermined by illegal immigrants, corrupt leaders, and deceitful reporters.

His victory represented just the latest upheaval in U.S. and global politics. Over the several decades I had been analyzing politics, there were a number of shocking shifts. In 1989 the Berlin Wall fell and the Cold War with the Soviet Union ended. Republicans upended five decades of Democratic rule in 1994, when they seized control of Congress and kept it for most of the next two decades. China has emerged as a global power and is flexing its economic and political might.

As if that were not enough, the twenty-first century generated another set of earthquakes that rocked the world. Technology innovation ushered in a digital world with tasks handled by robots and artificial intelligence. Same-sex marriage was legalized, and marijuana use no longer was considered a crime. Fundamentalism and terrorism surged in many parts of the world. Minorities and immigrants were rising in number in the United States, leading to predictions that whites would soon lose their majority status.

The result of all these developments is an American landscape infused with partisanship, polarization, and mutual intolerance. Simmering tensions over politics, economics, and culture have metastasized into an overarching us-versus-them environment. The idea of a melting pot, where people of different backgrounds and viewpoints fuse into peaceful coexistence, seems a quaint relic of another time.[6]

As these profound changes were unfolding, I had a front-row seat on the national transformation. I grew up in the 1960s and 1970s in a conservative community in rural Ohio. The church sermons there were full of fire and brimstone. Visiting my mother's local church in 2004, I heard Pastor Ralph Gutowski of the Fairhaven Community Church preach about the evils of abortion, gays, and evolution. "Abortion is immoral," he proclaimed. Gay lifestyles are a sign of decadence. Evolution runs contrary to the biblical story of creation. Western civilization is in decline because few people pay attention to the teachings of Jesus Christ.

At a personal level, this moralizing was awkward because sitting nearby was my gay brother, Ken, who could not believe his lifestyle was being attacked. My two sisters, Joanne and Shirley, were also in attendance; they had married local farmers and still lived in our hometown. They were Christian fundamentalists who were members of this congregation and generally supportive of what the minister was saying.

Most of the time, the four of us avoided politics and religion because we knew our family was at ground zero of the red state–blue state divide. Indeed, the social, economic, and political divisions associated with that conflict in many respects were the story of our lives. We had circled warily around one another for years, not wanting to lance the boil for fear it would lead to irreconcilable differences.

But with its pointed attack on my brother, Ralph's sermon was hard to ignore. The after-church lunch with my three siblings was tense. Over food, we tried to be on good behavior because my mother was seventy-nine and not in good health. It would turn out to be the last year of her life. We passed most of the lunch catching up on gossip and hearing what our local friends and relatives were doing.

When my mother was out of earshot, though, I broached the subject with Joanne. "What did you think of the sermon?" I asked. Knowing immediately what I was asking about, she said she had no idea the minister was going to address hot-button social topics. She was not happy Ralph had done so since he knew my brother was in town for a family reunion. Even though she generally agreed with the pastor's sentiments on social issues, she didn't appreciate his outspoken language that weekend.

My family had long been deeply conservative. When Shirley was researching our West family history, she was shocked to discover that our paternal grandfather had been a member of the Ku Klux Klan. As part of her effort, she had contacted every living member of my father's family. Most of my dad's twelve brothers and sisters were deceased, but a few still were alive.

Among her reminiscences, my aunt Eleanor indicated in a crisp and matter of fact tone that "the Ku Klux Klan came every weekend. Dad had an empty house and barn with a long lane. The Klan hid up there for secret meetings."[7] In that short burst, Aunt Eleanor turned our family history upside down. At first, I thought my aunt must be mistaken. When I was growing up, there had been no talk of the KKK. Perhaps my aunt was suffering a strange delusion as a result of her ripe old age. To be sure, my sister checked with one of our younger aunts. We both hoped Aunt Eleanor's memory would turn out to be mistaken. But my aunt Ruth confirmed the long-held family secret that Grandpa West was a Klansman, a topic no one previously had broached.

At one level, I should not have been surprised. My father's family came from a rural Indiana village of a few thousand with the ironic name of Liberty. The time my aunt recalled had been the heyday of the Indiana KKK. The Klan grew to great power and at one point controlled a large number of elected officials and judges in the Hoosier State. Many small Indiana communities around that time practiced conservative politics, and my family's hometown was no exception.

The community where I grew up was a far cry from the liberal university where I taught for more than twenty years. I was a political science and public policy professor at Brown University, one of the most progressive schools in America. At Brown, the political divide was not so much between Republicans and Democrats as between Democrats and socialists, as I liked to joke. It was not that socialists were numerous, but they were a noisy presence on campus.

The school was home to a series of famous Democratic offspring, such as John Kennedy Jr., Amy Carter, Bill Mondale, Kara Dukakis, and Alexandra Kerry. Chelsea Clinton didn't come to Brown, but the university was the runner-up to her eventual top choice, Stanford. Malia Obama also checked out Brown before settling on Harvard.

With its emphasis on social justice and progressive values, I teased my students that Brown was the Bob Jones University of the Left. As a sign of the school's political proclivities, a student newspaper poll revealed that 63 percent of undergraduates identified themselves as Democrats, 5 percent were Green Party adherents, 5 percent were Republican, 7 percent indicated other, and 20 percent identified as independent.[8] The outpouring of liberal sentiments in classroom discussions sometimes led me to practice affirmative action for conservatives to make sure their views were articulated.

Over time, the school's liberalism became quite flamboyant. One year, the Queer Alliance hosted a "Sex Power God" party that celebrated alternative lifestyles. Its organizers advertised the event outside the university and encouraged attendance from outside the Brown community. Through this external outreach, a young producer at Fox News's *The O'Reilly Factor* heard about the event. He raised the idea with his supervisors of attending the party with a video camera and taking footage of the revelers. The network gave him the go-ahead, and Fox producer Jesse Watters arrived at the party with camera in tow. He later would become infamous for exposés of liberal organizations around the country, get his own talk show on Fox TV, and be praised by President Trump for his tough-minded reporting.[9]

On November 14, 2005, salacious video from that campus party was shown nationwide on *The O'Reilly Factor*. The show was a favorite of conservatives, and it usually attracted several million viewers from around the country. As the footage showed provocative images from the party, O'Reilly interviewed his producer. Watters told him the "first thing I saw was this pure debauchery. Girls were falling down drunk all over the place. Most of the girls were wearing just panties, just bras."[10]

According to the young man, party attendees were engaging in sex in the bathroom. Although no alcohol was served at the party, in accordance with university rules, more than two dozen students drank so much alcohol before the party they required emergency medical treatment that night. Apparently, the libations loosened the inhibitions of some students. "I went down to the bathroom, was in a stall. I heard people having sex in the stall next to me," Watters said. "I did observe people having sex behind where the deejay was playing. There were guys kissing guys, girls making out with girls. . . . It was the wildest party I had ever been to."[11]

For O'Reilly, of course, this broadcast was completely hypocritical. In 2004 the darling of the right wing had been accused of sexual harassment by Andrea Mackris, a former Fox News producer.[12] She said he made lewd phone calls to her and attempted to start a romance. Many years later, in 2017, a series of staff settlements became public, and O'Reilly was forced off the air. For him to condemn college students for weekend revelry was especially unseemly, given his own poor personal behavior.

In 2008 I left the university for a vice president's job at the Brookings Institution, the leading think tank in the world. After World War II, its experts had been instrumental in devising the Marshall Plan that rescued European economies devastated by the war. Later, it developed innovative proposals to improve congressional budgeting and government operations. Now its researchers were working on issues of foreign policy, global development, economic studies, metropolitan policy, and governance studies.

Based in Washington, D.C., I was in the middle of the "swamp," as critics referred to the capital city. Located a dozen blocks north of the White House, Brookings was the epicenter of the Eastern Establishment and the place where business leaders, academics, and politicians came together to develop solutions to the world's leading problems. While there, I met presidents, senators, business magnates, and foreign dignitaries and had an inside look at the American power elite.

In this book, I draw upon my personal experiences growing up on a dairy farm in a conservative rural community, teaching at a liberal Ivy League university, and working in the heart of the D.C. establishment to analyze the political, economic, and cultural aspects of polarization. I use years of conversation with family and friends, correspondence, news articles, public opinion data, and social media posts to understand why liberals and conservatives are angry with each other and why there is so much mutual suspicion.

The nation's widespread polarization has made everyone uneasy. One of my high school friends told me, "Heard your interview on National Public Radio on June 16. Don't agree with a freakin' thing you said, but you're the only person whom I know personally that is of celebrity status."[13] My niece Laura attended a conservative religious university in the Midwest and explained her personal dilemma with me this way: "I've met many political science majors and all of them are impressed when I tell them you teach at Brown. That is, until they find out that you're a Democrat."[14]

ONE

MISTRUST

When I was writing my doctoral dissertation on the 1980 presidential campaign, I had no idea what a momentous election it would become. Ronald Reagan's triumph that year would usher in a transformative "Reagan Revolution" that would cut taxes, reduce domestic spending, alter social policy, and force the Soviet Union into an expensive arms race that would eventually bring down the Berlin Wall.[1]

But Reagan's actions seem mild compared with those of his successors. Over the next few decades, the country would gyrate from Reagan (and his successor, George H. W. Bush) to Bill Clinton to George W. Bush to Barack Obama to Donald Trump, and each leader would shift America in startling directions. This forty-year time period would become a tumultuous era in American history. Conflict during each administration would add to the country's profound mistrust and antagonism.

Each of these presidents provoked strong reactions from opponents. In speaking with family members, colleagues, and friends at various points in time, I could see polarization and partisanship intensify during each presidency. People reacted in highly personal ways to each leader's term in office. They did not trust any president from the opposite party, and they feared that he was destroying the America they loved. James Stewart notes that politics during this era became a "blood sport," with high levels of personal conflict and antipathy. That was an apt metaphor for this contentious time period.[2]

The Reagan Revolution

My father loved Ronald Reagan. A dairy farmer with thirty cows to milk twice a day, he wanted a Republican who was tough on defense, opposed to big government, and committed to morality, school prayer, and the sanctity of life. Reagan was an ideal leader for him because he understood the values of small-town America and did not talk down to ordinary folks the way, in his view, coastal elites and liberal politicians did.

Dad had several experiences that pushed him to the right. As a dairy farmer, he was subject to periodic and unannounced visits from milk inspectors, whose job was to ensure the quality and safety of the food supply. They would visit our farm and inspect our barns and dairy equipment. Anything that was unclean would be written up on a sheet and left in our milk house. If a farmer got flagged for the same violations several times in a row, the inspector had the power to close down the dairy operation and prevent the milk from being sold to processing plants. This was the nuclear option for milk inspectors, and sometimes they invoked it to make sure farmers took cleanliness seriously.

My father had regular run-ins with these overseers. They took positions he found hard to fathom. Early in my life, we raised both pigs and cows. This came to an end one day when a milk inspector informed us that pigs and cows could not graze on the same fields for fear of cross-species contamination.

On a family farm of 160 acres, it was impossible to separate these animals. We simply didn't have sufficient acreage to isolate our cows from the pigs. My father complained bitterly about this decision and thought it was an unwarranted intrusion into our business operations. It personified for him all that was wrong with government. "Milk inspectors should not tell farmers how to run their operations," he argued vehemently.

But the inspector was inflexible. "Sell the pigs and keep the cows," he warned, or vice versa. He didn't care which we did as long as one set of animals disappeared from our farm. My father's appeal of this draconian decision fell on deaf ears, and we sold the pigs and became dairy specialists.

These inspectors also objected to open milk cans. In the barn parlor where we milked the cows, we had buckets into which we would pour the milk. Inspectors insisted that these buckets have lids to keep dirt out. My father purchased a tall, stainless steel bucket with a perfectly fitting lid that he kept in our milk house so the inspector could see we were in compliance with the rules.

Of course, we never actually used this steel bucket, except to make large batches of fruit punch for family reunions. We continued to use the old buckets with no lids to carry our dairy milk as they were more convenient to use. Having lids on cans made it difficult to pour milk into the cans from our milking machines. But at least we were in technical compliance with the rules.

This is not to say that the inspectors had no legitimate concerns about the cleanliness of our dairy operation. When the cows walked into our milking parlor, they strode right past the open milk containers. One day, I saw a cow shit directly into a bucket full of milk. Asking my father what we should do, he walked over and scooped the fresh ball of manure out of the bucket with his bare hands. "Nothing," he said and dumped that bucket in with the rest of our milk. I made sure I did not drink any milk that night or for the next several days. Privately, I became a little more sympathetic to the government's position on food safety.

My mother was as conservative as my father. She knitted baby quilts for Birthright and the Pregnancy Care Center—organizations whose missions were to provide caring support to those with un-planned pregnancies. The groups would offer alternatives to abor-tion, such as adoption.

She furthermore was not a big fan of evolution as an explanation for natural phenomena. On one trip to Boston, my then-wife, Annie, and I took her to visit the Comparative Zoology Museum at Harvard University. It had a famous "glass flowers" exhibit in which German craftsman had created life-like models of numerous flowers showing all the details of each plant.

As we walked through the museum, we passed an exhibit on a prehistoric fish known as the coelacanth. This is thought to be the closest tie to the first amphibians, which crawled from sea to land during the Devonian stage 400 million years ago and thereby paved the way for human beings. Biologists love the fish because of its pre-historic roots and the fact that it is the only contemporary fish that dates back to that formative time period.

Seeing the description on evolutionary principles, my mother leaned over to Annie and said, "You know, I still don't believe all this evolution stuff." Annie taught in the department of ecology and evolutionary biology at Brown University, but she didn't say any-thing. She thought it best to stay quiet regarding her work on plant evolution. But we gave each other knowing looks about the clash of cultures. We understood about blue and red states long before that framework became popular in American politics.

Not surprisingly for a rural community, conservative organi-zations had a firm foothold in my hometown. When I was young, the local Women's Christian Temperance Union was overseen by a neighbor and fellow churchgoer. She railed against the dangers of alcohol and the need to outlaw liquor production. It was a grim irony that in later years her only son became an alcoholic, developed cir-rhosis of the liver, and died a premature death.

Other neighbors were active in the John Birch Society. This was a right-wing organization named after an American intelligence officer and Baptist missionary who was murdered by Chinese communists in 1945. Founded in 1958, the group's motto was "Less government, more responsibility, and—with God's help—a better world." It advocated a strong Judeo-Christian framework for American government and bitterly opposed the United Nations and other multilateral world organizations. The group fought the civil rights movement and opposed communism everywhere.[3]

My aunt Martha had a more local concern—the fluoridation of water. A registered nurse who lived in Cincinnati, she was convinced the government's plan to put fluoride in the water to prevent tooth decay, as recommended by expert medical panels, was a communist plot to undermine America. At any mention of fluoridation, she would go off on long tirades concerning her deep mistrust of the government. Her recipe for a long life was avoiding fluoridated water and giving herself a daily enema (what today is referred to as "colon cleansing").

Her views on fluoridation paralleled those of General Jack D. Ripper in the famous 1964 Cold War movie *Dr. Strangelove*. General Ripper explains to Group Captain Lionel Mandrake regarding the simultaneous dangers of communism and fluoridating water,

> I can no longer sit back and allow Communist infiltration, Communist indoctrination, Communist subversion and the international Communist conspiracy to sap and impurify all of our precious bodily fluids. . . . It's incredibly obvious, isn't it? A foreign substance is introduced into our precious bodily fluids without the knowledge of the individual. Certainly without any choice. That's the way your hard-core Commie works.[4]

As our only family member living in a large city, Aunt Martha also stood as our personal authority on racial matters. Our community was 100 percent white, but she worked with African Americans in several city hospitals, which gave her an experience none of us had. Yet she did not speak kindly about her minority colleagues and complained they were lazy. She was single and worried constantly about crime, especially attacks from those she called "the darkies."

I was perplexed at my aunt's racist attitudes and strange personal behaviors. I never understood why she hated African Americans and said such nasty things about them. As someone who had never met any racial minority before going to college, I found the the deep fears that many people felt about race hard to fathom.

When I went to graduate school at Indiana University, I decided to focus on campaigns for my doctoral dissertation. I loved political strategy and the way candidates mobilized voter support and built electoral coalitions. With the 1980 presidential contest coming up, I chose to study the tactics Republican and Democratic candidates used to win elections. If politics was the art of persuasion, I wanted to understand how they did it.

Using a grant from the National Science Foundation, I traveled around the country following the various candidates. On the Democratic side, I talked with top advisers to President Jimmy Carter, challenger Ted Kennedy, and upstart Jerry Brown. Kennedy was waging an effort to dethrone a sitting president from his own party. But his campaign was the most disorganized of all those I observed, and his staffers never seemed on top of their messaging or strategy.

Carter used all the perquisites of his office and cited the Iranian hostage crisis as the excuse for a "Rose Garden strategy" of not campaigning outside of the White House. Instead, he derided the personal character of Kennedy and broadcast ads about his family, while operatives snickered privately about Kennedy's womanizing and lack of family values.

One day at a Jerry Brown for President rally in New Hampshire, I sat next to rock star Linda Ronstadt. She was campaigning for her boyfriend Jerry, who was running for president. I took it as a bad sign for his candidacy when after his speech, many more people gathered around her than him.

Early in the campaign, I shook Ronald Reagan's hand at a small New Hampshire gathering. In spite of all those pictures of him chopping wood, my conclusion from this brief encounter was the guy did little physical labor as he had the softest hands of anyone I'd ever met. Later, during his presidency, I would see images of him working on his ranch and clearing brush, but judging from his uncallused hands, it clearly was not a frequent activity for him.

Along with a small crowd, I attended a party celebrating George H. W. Bush's announcement speech at his Virginia headquarters. While there, I met a distinguished-looking gentleman from Houston named Jim Baker who was running Bush's campaign. I didn't know much about him but was impressed with his smooth talk and smart insights into the political process. I had no idea he would emerge as one of President Reagan's top advisers and a future secretary of state.

Following Reagan's historic triumph, the Californian would preside over a dramatic transformation of the country's orientation. He would tilt the balance in American politics in a conservative direction. Along with his congressional allies, Reagan would cut taxes, reduce the federal bureaucracy, and slow the rate of growth in social welfare benefits.

He demonstrated the ability to forge an effective coalition of conservative Republicans, independents, and Democrats disenchanted with their party's stance on social issues and foreign policy. The chief executive was able to knit these individuals together into a movement that would force Democrats to shift to the center and allow Republicans to pursue an even more conservative policy agenda. The Soviet Union would be confronted by a massive military buildup that eventually bankrupted that country and led to the collapse of communism. This ended the Cold War and ushered in a period of American dominance in world affairs.

In contrast to my rural Ohio family, who were thrilled with Reagan's ascendancy, my Brown University colleagues hated Reagan and thought he represented the worst elements in American politics. Most of the people I knew there saw him as bigoted, uncaring, and stupid. In their minds he was a charlatan who beguiled voters with a folksy style but deep down was a dangerous and mean-spirited leader.

Seeking to organize public opposition to this administration, students came up with creative ways to criticize Reagan. One entrepreneurial pupil named Jason Saltzman, worried about the risk of nuclear war under the bellicose Reagan, organized a student referendum (Students for Suicide Tablets) asking the university administration to stock "suicide pills" for optional use in case the GOP president pushed the nuclear button.

If people were going to die from the blast, he reasoned, they might as well be allowed to take the painless way out. He explained that "college students have been silent about the arms race. But it's our world that is going to be destroyed." When asked about the suicide option, Jason indicated that he came up with the idea "to shock people into taking action. When you confront people with their own suicide, then they think about the suicidal nature of nuclear war."[5]

The vote was a symbolic expression in the middle of the Cold War of young people's worry about nuclear annihilation and the dangers of President Ronald Reagan's militaristic policy. Based on my childhood anxiety regarding the Cuban missile crisis, I definitely understood student fears about the destructive power of nuclear weapons.

Yet to the outside world, Brown University students were lunatics who thought nuclear war was imminent and wanted to commit suicide. Every major newspaper in the nation sent reporters asking what was happening at Brown and why the university's students were planning to take their own lives.

An editorial in the student newspaper opined that "a strong yes vote on the suicide pill referendum might rattle a lot of people's beliefs about college students. No, it would say, we are not just grade-grubbing pre-pro pre-yep resume packers. And yes, we do care about something beyond whether mommy will let us have the car this year."[6]

When the referendum passed with 60 percent of the student vote, university president Howard Swearer was forced to issue a statement saying Brown would not stock cyanide pills at the health center. Instead, the school would provide courses, forums, and lectures that would explore feelings about nuclear war.[7]

The Clinton Period

The Reagan-Bush years closed with a deep recession that gave an unknown governor from Arkansas named Bill Clinton the opportunity to usher Democrats back into power. With a deft political touch, Clinton rallied his party and won majorities in the House and Senate.[8] For a brief time, it looked as though the Reagan era represented a temporary blip in the political landscape, not a long-term transformation.

But conservatives had a plan to make sure Clinton did not succeed. He had a charming personality that liberals loved and conservatives hated. His supporters felt he connected well with typical voters and "understood their pain." He didn't talk down to people and was great at personalizing arguments in ways they could understand. Conservatives, however, saw him as a liberal charlatan who was fake and deceitful and had deep character flaws. They worked hard to make sure he was not successful.

Clinton made health care the centerpiece of his domestic agenda and argued it was time for the federal government to provide "health security" for the uninsured. As a so-called New Democrat, he felt that there were too many guns in America, and he hoped his Health Security Act would do for workers what Franklin Roosevelt's Social Security had accomplished in the 1930s. It would provide needed social benefits for the poor and cement the Democrats' grip on power.

Advising him on health care was Rhode Island resident Ira Magaziner, author of Brown's successful New Curriculum, which removed course distribution requirements. I knew Ira would either succeed or fail big on health care because he was a visionary who pushed bold ideas. He was never content with incremental reform.

In 1993, First Lady Hilary Clinton came to Brown University to promote the president's health care plan. I moderated the televised forum on health care reform, which featured Clinton along with Rhode Island's two senators (Claiborne Pell and John Chafee) and two representatives (Jack Reed and Ron Machtley).

The event was designed to show how the president's plan worked and what it would do for ordinary people. Following themes laid out by the White House, I interviewed several people from business about their health care problems. After hearing these tales of distress, Clinton explained how her husband's program would solve the problem, and the Rhode Island political leaders would chime in with their perspectives on the issue.

The event was like a rock concert. Six hundred people crowded into a university lecture hall, along with a gaggle of reporters. A husband and wife who ran a small trucking company in New Hampshire complained about the high cost of health care for their employees. After listening attentively to their story, the First Lady replied with great empathy, "This is how the president's plan would take care of that."

Seeing her up close, I saw she was smart, articulate, and knowledgeable about health matters. Throughout the evening, she repeated her constant refrain about "the president's plan" or "Bill's program." Not once did she talk about "my plan" or "the ideas I drafted," even though she and Ira were the major intellectual forces behind the proposal.

Despite the efforts of the president and First Lady, the Clinton health care proposal died ignominiously. Republicans attacked the plan as a federal takeover of health care and a big bureaucracy that would interfere with the private relationship between doctor and patient. Worried interest groups ran millions in television ads blasting the reform. A fictional couple named Harry and Louise became household names with their kitchen-table patter complaining about Clinton's effort. Along with Magaziner, the Clintons' bold initiative ended in embarrassing defeat.

As often happens in politics, every attempt at revolution stimulates a counterrevolution. Across the country, a growing movement began to gather intensity. Angry conservatives, upset over the president's health care reform, tax surcharges on the wealthy, and restrictions on assault weapon purchases, fought back.

During the 1994 midterm elections, conservative forces demonstrated that the Reagan Revolution was no blip. It was a movement with legs that would seize control of the House of Representatives for the first time in fifty years. This new force, known as the Gingrich Revolution, would make fire-brand Newt Gingrich Speaker of the House and put Democrats on the defensive for more than a decade.

While Reagan had pushed major changes through Congress, Gingrich and his fellow zealots brought a sharper edge to political conflict and polarized the nation along ideological lines. Reagan had been conservative, but Gingrich was a radical reformer. He saw himself as the leader who would carry Reaganism to new heights. His goal was to create what he called an "opportunity society" in which entrepreneurial talent would be rewarded and people who did well would not have to pay high taxes to the government to support public assistance and other programs for the poor and needy.

His bare-knuckle tactics helped the GOP gain control of Congress and use its new power to solidify a conservative coalition in American politics. Gingrich sought to divide the opposition party using wedge issues such as abortion, gay rights, and evolution. The new Speaker was not reluctant to use emotional rhetoric and divisive tactics to implement his policy agenda.

Republicans scored several legislative victories on tax cuts, welfare reform, and some entitlement cutbacks, yet they were unable to derail Clinton's reelection. They had nominated Senate Majority Leader Bob Dole to head their party slate. Dole's 1996 campaign confirmed my impressions of the Kansan's 1980 presidential bid: it was disorganized, strayed off message, and suffered from his close association with the divisive Gingrich. He wasn't warm and cuddly and did not have the political skills or rhetorical talent to defeat even a wounded Clinton.

The president coasted to an easy reelection but soon thereafter ended up in a personal predicament that would tarnish his legacy and undermine Democratic efforts to retain the presidency. During the dark days in 1995, when the government had been shut down and nonessential employees ordered home in a funding dispute with Republicans, a young intern named Monica Lewinsky was pressed into service to deliver food to the Oval Office. Flashing her thong at a president still reeling from his party's overwhelming defeat the previous year, the two began an affair that lasted a year.

When news leaked out about the relationship, the country was pitted in a red state–blue state divide that I knew all too well from my agrarian roots. Conservative midwesterners and southerners were outraged at adulterous oral sex in the White House, while coastal liberals decried the private behavior but claimed his personal misdeeds had no relevance for his job performance. Right after the news broke, my sister Joanne wrote me, "I don't think this will die down overnight. I think he's in trouble."[9]

Two months later, she still was upset about the scandal. "It's horrible all the jokes they say on late night television and everywhere else about him. It's an embarrassment to our country."[10] Conservatives thought liberals were being hypocritical in minimizing this ethical transgression, while liberals didn't understand how upsetting Clinton's personal behavior was to people in the Bible Belt. When the First Family had the family dog fixed, my hometown friends joked, Hillary had neutered the wrong Clinton.

The president was impeached by the House but retained in office by the Senate. Nearly everyone around the country seethed over the result. Liberals could not understand the millions spent investigating the president's private life, while conservatives were shocked the chief executive lied under oath about the affair. It spawned ugly feelings from everyone who followed the proceedings.

The following year, I got an up-close look at the scene of the affair. My former student Justin Coleman worked in the White House helping to manage the presidential paper flow. For years, he had been inviting me to come to Washington to have lunch in the White House dining room. I was in D.C. releasing the results of an e-government study and set up a lunch.

Before we dined, Justin showed me his office on the floor below the president's office. Although many years earlier I had taken the official tour of the White House, this was my first look at the inner sanctuary itself, the part not shown to tourists. In walking around that area, I was surprised at the close quarters within the West Wing. Befitting a place built in the nineteenth century, it was not a sleek office building with spacious offices and room to spread out. Space was at such a premium that nearly everyone virtually sat on top of one another. Justin shared a tiny cubbyhole with two co-workers.

Upstairs, I was surprised at the small size of the Oval Office. On television, it looked much more expansive than in person. Seeing the infamous desk and the carpet on which Lewinsky had performed oral sex on the president, I thought to myself that whoever became president in 2000 was going to have this carpet cleaned. When Republicans regained control of the White House that year, I was not surprised by the quiet announcement that newly elected president George W. Bush had replaced the entire Oval Office carpet.

In the end, Clinton's presidency barely dented the movement toward conservatism in America. After he shifted Democrats toward the political center, Republicans simply tacked further to the right. The gap between the two parties remained the same, only there was no true liberal voice anymore, and the GOP was able to pursue more radical policies well to the right of Democrats. The next president would demonstrate how to govern the country in a much more conservative direction.

Bush and the War on Terror

The Bush-Gore race of 2000 did nothing to ease the polarization and ill feelings unleashed by the Gingrich Revolution and Clinton's affair. With a strong economy, Vice President Al Gore should have won the campaign. Judging from past elections, Democrats were well positioned by the robust economic performance and budget surplus of the late 1990s.

Yet Gore suffered two major liabilities. First, he was not good at communicating with the general public and looked stiff next to the man he was attempting to succeed. There was none of the personal charm that had allowed voters to overlook his boss's imperfections. Bush had a folksy manner that appealed to the average person.

Second, Clinton's sex affair had energized the GOP base and elevated moral issues in American politics. Repeatedly, throughout the campaign, Bush promised to restore dignity to the office of the president. Everyone understood that the word "dignity" meant no more adulterous sex in the Oval Office. Although the campaign outcome remained in doubt for six weeks after Election Day while the courts reviewed Florida's voting disputes, Republicans in the end were aided by a friendly U.S. Supreme Court decision to stop counting contested votes.

If Reagan and Gingrich had been agents of change, both paled in comparison with a GOP led by an activist president with congressional majorities. Bush had campaigned on massive tax cuts, and he stayed true to his word. It was a tight vote, but the Republican Congress passed the biggest tax cut in the history of the country. Rather than secure Social Security, as Gore had proposed, much of that money went for tax relief targeted on the wealthy.

But it would be the extraordinary terrorist attacks on September 11, 2001, that marked the Bush presidency. I taught a 9 a.m. class that day on politics and mass media and had no idea of the horror that was unfolding in New York City and Washington, D.C. These were the days before mobile phones kept everyone constantly in touch with the outside world.

Returning mid-morning to my office after class, I was startled to find a dozen colleagues gathered around a television set watching the screen. Quickly, I learned that one World Trade Center building had collapsed and the other was about to fall; all this was broadcast live on national television before a horrified country. Writing to me the next day, Joanne said, "What a horrible thing . . . happened yesterday. . . . We will never forget that day. . . . I've never seen anything like this in my lifetime."[11]

In the short run, the nation pulled together in furor over the unjustified attack. Bush's job approval rating soared into the 80s. Virtually everyone except the most rabid liberals appreciated his firm leadership in the wake of the attacks. Expressions of sympathy poured into the country from all around the world. My mother said, "The President gave a wonderful speech the other night, but I think it will be impossible to catch all of these critters."[12]

Within the White House, Bush adviser Karl Rove formulated a new strategy for the administration. Rather than following the bipartisan strategy they had pioneered with the No Child Left Behind education legislation, which was co-written with liberal icon Ted Kennedy, the White House sought partisan advantage through this national crisis. The administration would launch a war on terrorism that evoked strong feelings from many corners of the country.

Moving quickly, the administration passed the so-called Patriot Act, which gave the government extraordinary power to gather intelligence information and compile data on phone calls, library book checkouts, and electronic communications. In foreign policy, Bush declared war on Afghanistan, the home of al Qaeda leader Osama bin Laden. American military forces quickly overthrew the country's Taliban leadership and installed a regime more friendly to the United States.

Around the same time, the president's hawkish advisers targeted Iraq as a nation they claimed harbored terrorism and weapons of mass destruction. After a vote in the Senate supporting military actions, U.S. forces invaded. Quickly, American troops overran Baghdad and took control of the country. Saddam Hussein was forced into hiding and was eventually captured and executed. Bush flew to an aircraft carrier in the region and spoke under a sign declaring "Mission Accomplished."

That sign turned out to be woefully premature. The president and his team thought Iraq was going to be like Eastern Europe after the Iron Curtain fell: get rid of the dictator, they assumed, and there would be rejoicing in the streets. Before long, capitalism and democracy would flourish, and Bush would be the hero who transformed the Middle East and brought democracy to that troubled region.

Of course, what that optimistic scenario neglected was the generations of ethnic, religious, and class conflict in Iraq. As soon as Saddam Hussein was gone, many Iraqis reverted to their Sunni, Shiite, or Kurdish roots and pursued long-standing grievances against their fellow country people.

Given the history of ethnic hatred, the Iraq War dragged on with extensive violence inside that nation and became a contentious issue within the United States. Democrats accused the administration of lying and deceit in getting the country involved in an unwinnable war based on a manufactured rationale, while Republicans complained that Democrats only wanted to "cut and run" and were soft on terrorism.

In 2006 the country repudiated Bush and his Iraq War policies. In a stunning reversal, Democrats regained majority control of the House and Senate. For the first time in twelve years, Democrats would be in control of Congress. The Reagan-Bush-Gingrich revolution seemingly was over, and Democrats had a platform from which to pursue a more progressive agenda.

For me, our country's polarization between red and blue states on Bush and the Iraq War hit very close to home. My family remained sharply divided when it came to politics. Ken was no fan of the Bush presidency. He sent me liberal jabs that read "January 20, 2009, the end of an error," "Bush. Like a Rock. Only Dumber," and "When Fascism Comes to America, It Will Be Wrapped in a Flag, Carrying a Cross." And in a precursor to Donald Trump's chants about Hillary Clinton in 2016, he passed along a popular Democratic meme about Bush, calling for "jail to the chief."

Not to be outdone, Shirley sent me a birthday card from the Midwest showing a smiling picture of "President Hillary Clinton" sitting in the Oval Office. On the next page, the punch line announced, "See? There are some things scarier than turning a year older." Understanding that my political predispositions didn't match her own, Shirley added her own personal note to the birthday card: "Happy Birthday, Darrell! I'm sure you didn't find this card as funny or scary as we did!!!"

During this time, my brother-in-law Tim told me that he had discovered definitive proof in the Bible that God was a Republican. When I asked for the evidence, he referred me to the New American Standard Bible verse from Ecclesiastes 10:2, which read that "a wise man's heart directs him toward the right, but the foolish man's heart directs him toward the left."

I was not surprised at our family schism over politics and religion. When I went home to Ohio, I heard rantings about the dangers of terrorism, the virtue of Bush, and the importance of firm moral values in national policymaking. Back at Brown, nearly all my students and colleagues hated Bush, blamed him for an unpopular war, and thought the administration was filled with liars. A number believed Bush should be impeached or tried for war crimes.

All of the political conflict illustrated the enormous gulf that existed between midwestern and East Coast communities. One Christmas, we went to Shirley's house for dinner. During the course of the meal, someone brought up the issue of Iraq and George W. Bush's handling of the war. My two brothers-in-law, Jim and Tim, gave a rousing defense of Bush's policies and said how unfair it was that Bush was being criticized for American troops who tortured foreign prisoners.

I was astounded that anyone in my family would justify the use of torture. Not only would this violate the New Testament dictum to love they neighbor, but also there was the logistical problem that if we torture, how can we condemn other nations that do the same thing or expect them not to do the same to us? As Annie listened to this conversation, she could not believe what she heard. Knowing my Ohio family was very religious, she posed a sly question. "What would Jesus say about torture?" she plaintively asked.[13]

Much to our surprise, though, both of my brothers-in-law who were devout Christians said that Jesus would torture terrorists and Iraqi prisoners because those people were barbaric. Jim made the further point that Jesus would "use nuclear weapons in Iraq and get rid of the whole damn country." This spurred a vigorous dinner debate over whether Jesus would or would not use nuclear weapons in Iraq. My nephew Jeff took the more progressive view that Jesus would not torture prisoners and would not use nuclear weapons, while several others argued he would.

These family arguments were illuminating and helped me understand conservative viewpoints. In 2004 this exposure enabled me to see why at a time of continuing worry over terrorism, President Bush was likely to be reelected. The economy was strong, voters remained concerned about terrorism, and Bush ran a stronger campaign than his Democratic rival, John Kerry.

Having some grasp of midwestern sentiments also helped me in my role as a national media commentator. When peace activist Cindy Sheehan protested Bush's war policies, Bill O'Reilly, of the Fox News show *The O'Reilly Factor*, invited me onto his program to discuss what he saw as media liberalism in her favor.

O'Reilly started speechifying from the beginning of the interview. "Most of the media in this country doesn't like President Bush. It was obvious in the presidential campaign. . . . You have the most radical elements in the country controlling Cindy Sheehan. . . . Why do you think the press is so overwhelmingly on her side?" he asked nonchalantly.[14] It wasn't an actual question, more a statement of his own personal opinion.

I agreed with him that Sheehan was getting favorable treatment from the national press but disagreed with his attribution of responsibility to a liberal media. I set up an alternative reason for the coverage: "The media have sided with Cindy Sheehan just because public opinion drives the press coverage. We've seen public support for the war starting to decline. And when you look at past wars, when the polls start to turn against a war, oftentimes the press coverage follows," I argued. "Cindy Sheehan is the perfect antiwar symbol. She's a mother who's grieving for her lost son."[15]

Through all these family, university, and media conversations, it was clear that dangerous forces were being unleashed in American politics. The country was becoming polarized, and it was becoming harder and harder to have reasoned discussions of national events. People were doubting their adversaries and feeling they were not trustworthy. The Obama presidency would elevate these sentiments to new heights.

The Obama Years

Two years before Barack Obama's election, many people thought Hillary Clinton would be the next president. She had strong support from the Democratic establishment, while he was a young and relatively unknown Illinois senator. He had given an inspiring speech at the 2004 Democratic convention, but that seemed to be his only credential.

But in 2006, Clinton returned to Brown University to speak at a forum on women's leadership, and her visit revealed the deep problems she faced within the progressive base. Since I introduced the forum, I got to spend time with her before the event. Knowing I was a pollster and political analyst, she asked me how the U.S. Senate race in Rhode Island was shaping up. I told her I thought the incumbent, Republican senator Lincoln Chafee, was going to lose the general election to Sheldon Whitehouse, and 2006 would be a big Democratic year. She said she hoped so because even though she liked Chafee personally, he represented one of the seats standing in the way of Democratic control of the Senate.

We joked about the fact that two of her past press secretaries had been former students of mine: Lisa Caputo had worked for her in the White House, and Karen Dunn had been her Senate press secretary.

Both had moved on to other jobs, but Mrs. Clinton recalled how great Brown students had been in her office. "They are so wonderful," she cooed. "You always can count on good students coming out of Brown."

When she came out to speak, Senator Clinton received a hero's welcome. There was a standing ovation at the beginning and rounds of applause thereafter, especially when she criticized the Bush administration for talking tough but not taking effective action to solve the nation's problems.

Midway into her speech, though, several students and community activists began heckling her at the top of their voices. "Is it leadership to support the war?" one man shouted. Others unfurled an anti-Iraq War banner that proclaimed her "Clinton War Senator" in honor of her votes to approve the Iraq War and provide funding for its continuation.[16]

Although Senator Clinton ignored the protesters and continued with her speech, it was a significant moment in her presidential aspirations. The protests would signal the unease and dissatisfaction her 2008 presidential campaign would unleash within the progressive community. Activists across the country would accuse Hillary Clinton of not being liberal enough. In most places throughout the Midwest, people considered her far too liberal to serve as president. Many of my students, though, thought she wasn't critical enough of Bush's foreign policy.

In the days after the speech, protesters justified their attempt to shout down Clinton through rationales that sounded totalitarian. Writing in the *Brown Daily Herald*, International Socialist Organization representatives Alden Eagle and Shaun Joseph argued that "when the ordinary machinery of democracy produces no results, it is your right to disrupt the operation of tyrannical government by any means necessary. When anyone encroaches on the civil rights of others, as Clinton did when she voted for the USA Patriot Act, their own rights are forfeit."[17]

While Senator Clinton was speaking at Brown, former president

Bill Clinton was across town having dinner at Providence Prime restaurant with several political friends.[18] A journalist friend of mine who was at the dinner noticed a beautiful woman, wearing a low-cut dress, go up to Clinton to request an autograph, which the former president gave. A few moments later, he noticed Clinton talking and laughing with someone else. He later asked that person what the two had been discussing. He was told that right after the woman left, Clinton leaned over and asked whether his friend thought the woman's breasts were real.[19] Less than a decade after his own impeachment over lying about an affair, Clinton had not given up his eye for women.

Later that year, I got a chance to meet Senator Barack Obama and see the contrast with Clinton. We ran a lecture series featuring prominent leaders, and he agreed to speak. However, his flight from Newark, New Jersey, got canceled and he had to rent a car and drive himself to Providence. He showed up by himself in the rental car, several hours late, but no one had left the auditorium. If the Brown community had a certain unease with Hillary Clinton's muscular foreign policy, they idolized Senator Obama.

At the lecture, he talked about the importance of hope in American politics and repeatedly received standing ovations from the crowd. "Cynicism is the lazy way out—you guys are too young to feel that way," he announced. "When we get in trouble in democracy, it's because nobody's paying attention."[20]

My only personal regret at this gathering was that before we went on stage, Obama asked to use a bathroom. Because we were running so late, I made up some excuse that there wasn't one nearby. Looking back on that, I could not believe how inconsiderate my behavior was. Every time now when I have to go to the bathroom and don't have access to a restroom, I recall my disrespectful treatment of Obama and assume my bladder discomfort represents bad karma over my personal rudeness.

In 2009, after he had been elected president and I had moved to the Brookings Institution, I got invited to the White House to attend the unveiling of the Obama-Biden Middle Class Taskforce. It was designed to help people hurting from the Great Recession and strengthen economic prosperity among average workers. At the end of his speech, he shook many hands and worked his way back to the row where I was seated. I shook his hand and reminded him we had met at Brown right before he had gone onto Tim Russert's television show, *Meet the Press*, to announce he was running for president. Obama remembered the visit and joked that "that is where this all started."[21] Fortunately for me, he didn't seem to remember the bathroom denial.

While Obama delighted my liberal friends with his progressive values and being the first African American president, most of my Ohio family and friends seethed at his victory. Nearly all of them hated him and thought he had no respect for mainstream values. When Joanne heard I was going to the White House, she told me to "talk some sense into them." My nephew Doug was even more blunt. He asked me to tell Obama to "stop being an idiot."[22]

Most of my conservative friends condemned his economic stimulus package and thought his Affordable Care Act would destroy individual choice in health care. One of my hometown friends named Cindy wrote on my Facebook page after I advertised a radio appearance dealing with Martin Luther King Day that "you can thank the Obamas for the racial divide. . . . In my 58 years of life, the 8 years he was in office is the most divided this country has ever been."

Doug, the husband of one of my nieces, informed me of the only upside he saw to the Obama presidency. Realizing that talk of gun control under Obama would drive up the prices of guns and ammunition, he invested in them right after the election and then sold later when prices were much higher, making a profit. I was impressed at his clear foresight on how rural America would respond to a liberal Democrat in the White House and his skill at monetizing that insight.

His uncanny perception turned out to be just the tip of the iceberg. Having an African American leader sparked an intense backlash from many quarters around the country. Many whites didn't like having a black president. Some Christians complained that Obama was a secret Muslim who would sell American interests down the river. Republicans in Washington voted against everything Obama proposed, while their base cheered their obvious partisanship and obstructionism.

Yet the strangest response came from New York real estate billionaire Donald Trump. He argued that Obama was not an actual American because he had not been born in the United States. In a move that many at the time dismissed as vaudeville behavior, Trump demanded to see the original copy of Obama's Hawaii birth certificate—not the short form or a photocopy but the actual long form.

Obama did not take this attack very seriously. At the White House Correspondents' Dinner in 2011, he joked, "No one is happier—no one is prouder—to put this birth certificate matter to rest than The Donald. And that's because he can finally get back to focusing on the issues that matter: like did we fake the moon landing?"[23] But Trump had the last laugh. Through this and other efforts to undermine President Obama, he would become the new star of the Republican party.

Shock and Awe under Trump

Trump ran an unconventional campaign for the presidency. In a scene that was considered a publicity stunt, he came down a long escalator at Trump Tower in New York City in 2015 and announced he was running for president. The country was in crisis, he intoned, and beset by crime and violence.

At first, few people on the East Coast took Trump seriously. He was saying outrageous things and had a checkered past in terms of his behavior with women, investors, and the media. He had been married three times, in two cases to immigrants, and comedians joked his proclivity for foreign women "was because no American would take the job."

During the campaign, Trump vanquished one Republican rival after another. He assigned mocking monikers to them: "low-energy Jeb," "little Marco," and "lyin' Ted." When Lindsay Graham made critical remarks about Trump, the billionaire publicized Graham's personal cell phone number on national television, forcing the South Carolinian to get a new number.

After he gained the GOP nomination, he turned his attention to the Democratic nominee, Hillary Clinton. Seeking to undermine her credibility and raise her negatives as high as his own, he dubbed her "crooked Hillary." She should not be trusted, he proclaimed, because she used a private e-mail server and had been secretary of state when American diplomats were killed in Benghazi, Libya. Her charitable foundation, the Clinton Foundation, had accepted foreign money. Trump encouraged his supporters to chant "Lock her up!" at his rallies.

His victory revealed deep divisions across the communities where I had lived. In Preble County, Ohio, where I had been raised, Trump won 75 percent of the vote, compared with 21 percent for Clinton.[24] In Washington, D.C., where I currently live, Clinton trounced Trump by an astonishing 87-point margin (91 percent to Trump's 4 percent of the vote).[25] And at Brown University, where I had taught for many years, an October 2016 poll of undergraduates undertaken by the *Brown Daily Herald* found 85 percent supported Clinton while a paltry 1.8 percent favored Trump.[26]

Eighty percent of white evangelicals voted for Trump, but the billionaire's victory also galvanized many into intense opposition.[27] The day after his inauguration, millions of women marched on Washington in an extraordinary display of discontent toward his administration. People who I knew who hadn't been particularly political showed up to march.

At Brookings, one of my colleagues sued Trump for ethics violations at his business properties. Others drew parallels to the rise of Adolf Hitler in Germany during the 1930s and worried that Trump's scapegoating of adversaries and bellicose behavior would move the

United States toward a calamitous future. Still others called on voters to boycott the Republican Party on grounds that it represented "a threat to democratic values and the rule of law."[28]

My second wife, Karin, was German and was particularly concerned about Trump's authoritarian tendencies. As a student of her own country's history, she appreciated that "the unthinkable can happen" and that sometimes people don't realize what is going on until it is too late. Her fears about democracy were not assuaged when President Trump criticized Democrats for being "un-American" and "treasonous" in not applauding his comments about low unemployment during a State of the Union address.[29]

After Nikolaus Cruz killed seventeen students in a Florida school in 2018, my brother Ken shared a Facebook post from the liberal group Occupy Democrats. It said, "He is not a Muslim. He is not in ISIS. He is a terrorist with an AR-15. We don't need a stupid wall to keep us safe. We need REAL GUN CONTROL!"[30]

Many of my hometown relatives and friends, though, did not share that view. My high school friend Bob wrote on Facebook, "It's amazing how our media can make random acts of terror, foreign or domestic, into a political agenda within hours of the occurrence. Keep your guns, folks. You're going to need them."[31] Another friend named Carolyn shared a Facebook missive that said, "Dear God, Why do you allow so much violence in our schools? Signed, a Concerned Student. Dear Concerned Student, I'm not allowed in school. God."[32]

Most of my high school friends and relatives who lived in the Midwest voted for Trump. It wasn't that they were especially thrilled with him. As moralists, they disliked his womanizing and the fact he had been married three times. Shirley did not approve of his supposed affair with pornography star Stormy Daniels. My sister shared the sentiment expressed by Robert Jeffress of First Baptist Church in Dallas that "evangelicals knew they were not electing an altar boy. Forgiveness is part of the evangelical gospel message. We all are sinners."[33]

But the prospect of a Hillary Clinton presidency was completely unacceptable to them. The former senator was dishonest and not trustworthy, they felt, and would take America in the wrong direction. Shirley explained to me one day, "I wish the liberal media would accept Trump and quit trying to find something to impeach him on. Obama and Clinton did worse and nobody said a word."

A year into his presidency, I asked Joanne why she liked Trump, and she told me, "He thinks outside the box." By that, she meant he took unconventional positions and did not necessarily accept the perceived wisdom of past approaches. Shirley meanwhile felt the news media were not giving him a fair chance. "The media are corrupt," she argued. But good things were happening under Trump, she felt, because "God is using him."

Ken did not share this view of the Trump presidency. He forwarded a Bette Midler tweet that said, "The *Washington Post* says in his 1st year as Prez, Trump made 2,140 false claims & this year he's more than doubled that in just 6 months. In a way it's a miracle. Nobody's ever seen that much bullshit come out of a horse's ass."[34]

On the evening of his 2018 State of the Union address, I asked my Facebook followers a simple question I knew would trigger intense divisions: "Do you think Trump has made America great again?" I was not disappointed when nearly 150 people responded.[35] From my more liberal friends, I received the following comments:

"Trump has made America grate again . . . as in our teeth." *(Kelly, a Rhode Island resident)*

"He's made America hate again." *(Dan, a former graduate student)*

"I feel the need to apologize for being American." *(Liz, a Rhode Island resident)*

"He is slowly but surely destroying our country and our democracy." *(Nancy)*

"I refuse to accept him ever!! I do have to move on from the hangover left from realizing 63 million people voted for this moronic fool." (*Mary, a Rhode Island friend*)

"He's made Amerika, the Kleptocracy more potent." (*Jonathan, a Rhode Island resident*)

"He will aid in the decline of America and of democracy." (*Tom, my brother-in-law*)

"This is horrifying to watch. Fear and hate mongering, and shameless plugging of HOW MANY families to push his hatred agenda!" (*Kim, a former Brookings colleague*)

"Our democratic institutions and norms, the rule of law, respect for science, and basic civility and decency have been under constant siege from a pathological narcissist, liar, and race baiter in the White House. The country is more divided than at any time since the Civil War, [there is] creeping Erdogan/Putin-esque authoritarianism, and continuing obsequiousness towards the Kremlin." (*Chip, a former Brown University student*)

"He sullies everything that's great about this country, starting with the rule of law and respect for all people." (*a D.C. colleague*)

"He changes his mind daily, he's a bully, our nation has not been so divided since the civil war." (*Joe*)

"He's turned the Republicans into blind fools, but that wasn't hard." (*Matthew, a friend from Paris*)

"I continue to be embarrassed. The man has absolutely no class; how could we have elected him to run our country?" (*Alison*)

"The trope of American greatness is ethnocentric at best, and has the potential to be twisted into ideas that are downright creepy." (*Laurel, a Rhode Island friend*)

"His hateful tweets speak for themselves as they imply that he is the President of mostly his base of supporters, not of the entire country." (*Mitch, a Brookings friend*)

But at the same time, many of my conservative friends stood behind the president. They responded to Trump's speech in the following manner:

"He reduced unemployment almost as much in his first year as Obama did in any of his last five." (*Tim*)

"I like Trump and he's doing exactly what I had hoped he would do. Everybody liberal-minded hates him and most hard working Americans love him. I say keep up the good work." (*Bob, a childhood friend*)

"Greatest State of the Union speech I have ever seen. . . . Like him or not he was measured and clearly set the agenda . . . and the economy is moving. The haters are going to hate." (*Mike, a Rhode Island Republican*)

"I don't like the man but I like the fact that he is not a status quo politician and that he's doing exactly what we elected him to do." (*Scott, a childhood friend*)

"Better than it was under Obama." (*Steve, a Rhode Island conservative*)

"Great job. . . . Stuff gets done." (*Lorna*)

"I learned a long time ago that you can't reason with liberals. They simply don't care about the facts. Trump is making America great again and in just one year has corrected much of the harm done to our country by the previous, communist minded administration." (*Scott, a childhood friend*)

"Mostly last night I was disgusted with the Dems. I understand they don't like Trump but to not stand for our military?? Not to stand for the DACA kids? Infrastructure which is their baby? Pelosi looked like she ate a lemon." *(Carolyn, a childhood friend)*

"We are guilty of allowing others to take advantage of our generosity. The media was biased even before Trump arrived on the political scene." *(Scott, a Rhode Island GOP official)*

"On his way. Takes time to fix 8 years of screw-ups." *(Scott, a childhood friend)*

"He has done some things to make this country better, I wouldn't say great. If he knew how to treat people with love and tact maybe he could accomplish a lot more." *(Richard, a childhood friend)*

"Wow, Darrell. You need a bunch of new friends." *(Tim, a childhood friend)*

Almost all of these comments came from people I had known well at various points in my life, but they were remarkable in their range and intensity of sentiments. Trump elicited strong reactions from all parts of the political spectrum. There were clear disagreements based on where people lived, what they did, and their political viewpoints. But the comments were heartfelt in conveying their anger at the opposition.

Around that time, my Ohio friend Cindy wrote me an impassioned e-mail complaining about Democrats: "Obamacare should have never even been created. I know from one of my own family members it is NOT affordable. She still has no insurance and pays the government a penalty. In my eyes that's our own government is robbing us." Continuing, she asked me, "Why were the Obamas and the Clintons never investigated for what I feel was criminal?"

From her perspective, Trump was far preferable to the Democrats.

She said, "I believe God has put President Trump in office. He has used all kinds of people to do His work. He did not only use so called 'good' people. These facts are backed up in the Holy Bible." She closed by noting, "None of this is aimed directly at you in any way. We can just agree to disagree. Make America Great Again."

TWO

ECONOMIC FRUSTRATIONS

The past few decades have seen not only substantial political gyrations but also major economic disruptions. Agricultural jobs have declined, manufacturing positions have moved abroad, new business models have arisen based on temporary workers, technology has disrupted entire industries, and there has been wage stagnation among the middle class and an increase in income inequality. All these developments have produced a sharp rise in public fear, anxiety, and anger.

Befitting a period of tremendous change, Americans are divided regarding who is to blame for their economic distress. For average workers, there have been no actual wage increases beyond inflation in thirty years.[1] Progressives use this information to deride Wall Street and big business as being unfair and greedy and say those institutions have stifled middle-class prosperity.

In response, conservatives cite big government, high taxes, and overregulation as the culprits. My friend Linda posted a Halloween joke on Facebook illustrating this interpretation. It showed an adult on his doorstep telling young people, "Look how much candy you have! I'm going to take half and give it to the kids too lazy to go trick or treating for themselves!" The trick-or-treaters replied, "Oh crap, a democrat."[2]

One of the reasons there has been so much conflict in past decades is the tremendous disparity in economic results based on education and geography. My hometown friends did not fare well during this period, while the students who populate elite universities went on to prosperous careers. Understanding the financial gulf between the hinterland and coasts is crucial to understanding why hyperconflict has escalated.

The Decline of Agriculture

One part of the dramatic shift in the American economic landscape has been the decline of the agrarian workforce.[3] In 1800, 83 percent of Americans worked on a farm. That number dropped to 55 percent in 1850, 38 percent in 1900, 12 percent in 1950, and 2 percent in 2000. By that point, there were around 4.5 million farmers out of the country's 246 million people.[4]

During this transition, companies like Monsanto, Dow, Tysons, and Archer Daniels Midland became preeminent as farmers expanded their tillage. But with the tiny number of farmers, neither Democrat nor Republican lawmakers had many electoral incentives to address the plight of small-time growers. There were few votes to be gained from talking about agriculture as political power shifted to urban and suburban areas.

Sometimes, presidents even undertook actions that hurt farmers. For example, in 1973 Nixon imposed a food embargo against the sale of soybeans to Japan that harmed agricultural producers. In 1980 Democratic president Jimmy Carter placed a grain embargo on trade with the Soviet Union after it invaded Afghanistan. President Trump imposed tariffs on aluminum and steel in 2018, and China responded by raising tariffs on agricultural products. Anticipating the negative economic ramifications for agrarian Trump voters, Ken sent me a liberal meme saying, "Dear Red State Farmers for Trump, You're Fucked."

But later, after Trump freed up government money to bail out these very same farmers, my brother was angry at what he saw as conservative hypocrisy. He e-mailed me his view, saying, "I just find it incredible that the $12 billion aid package to farmers is not considered welfare by those receiving it. They consider handouts to the poor and needy as unjust but this is welcome?"[5]

In reality, neither party has been very helpful to farmers economically, but for rural dwellers, the saving grace of the Republican Party was that its values were closer to theirs on cultural and social issues.[6] People in my hometown did not like the Supreme Court's outlawing school prayer, did not believe women should have the right to an abortion, and intensely disliked the country's slide toward secularization. These issues locked rural folks into the Republican Party despite its leaders' failure to advance their economic status.

Even after agriculture went into a steep decline, most Americans had no appreciation of the economic and social devastation inflicted on rural areas because their lives were so far removed from those locales. After World War II, there had been a mass migration to the cities, and farm living became a lost memory for most Americans.

But that was not the case with me. I grew up in the country, and most of my family and childhood friends still lived in rural communities. On my yearly returns to Ohio, I could see the difficult health and financial circumstances that many people faced.

In many respects, country living was rigorous and demanding. There was lots of physical labor, and work had to be undertaken until the job was complete. It didn't matter the time of day or weather condition. You stayed until the cows were milked and the crops harvested.

When I was young, a typical day meant getting up before dawn. One of my regular tasks was to gather our cows from the field. Invariably, the creatures would be at the far end of the pasture. I would walk several hundred yards into the field hoping the cows would not take too long in returning to the barn. Our herd was "free range" long before it became a fashionable food-marketing technique.

In the winter, the cows stayed in the barn and were fed chopped corn harvested during the fall. This meant entering a narrow, cobweb-filled passageway along the exterior wall of our silo and climbing thirty-five feet of iron rings to the top. The space was just big enough that a small person could ascend the rings. Economically minded midwesterners don't like to build things any larger than necessary.

When we reached the apex, we would climb into the silo through a two-by-two-foot hole and use a large pitchfork to throw the silage down the exterior passageway. After shoveling the morning's allotment through the window, we went back down to the base of the silo and carried the chopped corn outside to the cow troughs. We would do this one fork load at a time, and it would take considerable time to feed the entire herd twice a day.

Once we got the cows to the barn, we would bring them into our milking parlor in small groups. There was a line of iron stanchions, one for each cow. We would direct each animal into the stanchion with ground corn feed as the incentive and lock the metal stanchion around its neck so it couldn't back out. While the cows were soothed by food, we would wash the manure off their udders and attach rubber suction tubes to each cow's four teats. The electric milking machines simulated the grip of the human hand, and over the course of five or ten minutes, the suction pressure would draw the milk out of each cow.

The only problem in using milking machines was we had to lean close to the cow right in front of their hind legs. If it had been raining outside and the cow was soaked, we got wet. If it was ninety degrees, the close encounter with the cow was stultifyingly hot. If the temperature was zero degrees, as it often was during my midwestern youth, our hands nearly froze.

The job of milking cows was cold in the winter, hot in the summer, and dirty and dangerous all year round. Since cows were eating while we milked them, they sometimes would get startled when someone came up beside their hind legs to clean their udders. When a cow is surprised, her first impulse is to kick the offending party, so I quickly learned the virtue of managing their expectations. I had to warn cows in advance about impending moves so they would not kick me. This was a life skill that came in handy later in my life as an academic administrator. When I violated the expectations rule with colleagues, they generally reacted the same way our cows did.

Although many of my childhood classmates lived on farms, most of their parents no longer milked cows. The number of dairy farms in America had dropped to 334,000 in 1980 and eventually would decline to 60,000 by 2006.[7] By the late twentieth century, half of the milk produced in America would come from farms with herds of more than 500 cows. Even rural people in my hometown thought the work of the small-town dairy farmer was too demanding as there was no time off from the twice-a-day grind.

In the spring, there were fields to be prepared and crops to be planted. When the corn rose to around six inches, we had to drive tractors with cultivators attached to them that dug out the weeds without damaging the rising crop. It was work that required constant attention to the corn row. This was not a place for someone who suffered from attention-deficit disorder. What made the job so difficult was the tediousness of driving a tractor, row by row, across the entire field. It might take half a day or so to finish a single field, and if we let our minds wander too far, we would plow out the newly planted corn.

The dirtiest and hottest job was baling hay. This took place in July and August, when the temperatures were well above ninety degrees. We cut the grass, alfalfa, and timothy that made good winter feed for our cows. After it baked for a couple of days in the hot sun, while hoping that no rain would damage the hay, we would drive a tractor and mechanical rake that would turn the cut hay into row after row of winnowed grasses.[8]

At this point, the serious labor would begin. My father drove a tractor with a hay baler attached to it. The baler would draw up the rows of hay, combine it into a rectangular mass that was three feet long, one foot wide, and two feet deep, and place twine around each bale so someone could move the bale. Each bale weighed well over fifty pounds. A wagon was attached to the end of the baler, and one by one, bales of hay would come out of the machine, about once every ten seconds.

My task on the wagon was to stack the bales two rows wide and five rows high. The bales had to be intertwined neatly so they would not fall off the wagon when we were driving along bumpy hills. It was back-breaking work during the hottest months of the summer. Even in gym workouts later in life, I never sweated as much as I did during those summers baling hay.

After the wagon was loaded with around eighty bales of hay, it would be driven to the barn for storage. Our barn had an elevated loft above our milking parlor where the hay was stored for wintertime use. Unloading the wagon involved placing each bale on an elevator and sending the hay from the wagon up to the second-floor loft.

Two or three people would stand in the hay mow taking bales off the elevator and stacking them in the barn. If the heat in the fields seemed unbearable, the barn was even worse. There was no ventilation in the mow, just dirt, dust, and human sweat. Anyone who had allergies or suffered from hay fever would never have survived this job. It generally took thirty minutes to unload one wagon of hay. When we finished that task, there were more loads coming from the field.

A good day of haying meant loading and unloading ten wagons, often starting at 9 a.m. and finishing around 7 p.m. At the end of that day, our arms were scratched from the hay. We were occasionally surprised when, turning a bale over and putting our hands into the twine, we would discover a half-dead field snake that had been picked up by the baler. In their already damaged condition, the reptiles were not happy about being trapped in a bale of hay.

In the fall, there were barns to be cleaned and manure spread on the fields. The job meant riding a tractor while right behind, a whirling contraption threw the manure off the back of the spreader. At least, that was the theory. In my experience, around 10 percent of the manure flew forward onto me, rather than behind the spreader, where it was supposed to land. After a few experiences with spreading manure, I learned the virtue of wearing a jacket with a hood attached to it so the flying manure did not get on me. Even in the intense summer heat, I always wore a hooded jacket when spreading manure.

In small towns across America, farm life was challenging, but it created a tremendous sense of community. People had a purpose that fulfilled them. Often in conjunction with religion, agricultural life made individuals feel they were contributing to a larger good. What could be more satisfying than feeding other people?

When agricultural jobs disappeared, entire communities were disrupted, leaving a major void in the lives of rural dwellers. The disappearance of agrarian work uprooted traditional ways of living and created considerable discontent. People longed for the strong sense of community well-being that came with this vocation.

By the early 1970s, around the time I graduated from high school, only 13.5 percent of agrarian sons stayed on the farm, down from 60 percent in 1900.[9] The ones who persisted would endure many economic hardships in following years. While coastal Americans prospered, farmers saw their livelihoods vanish and poverty and opioid abuse afflict their communities.

Lost Manufacturing Jobs

As agriculture lost its luster, manufacturing became a logical transition for many in the Midwest. Country people knew how to work hard and were reliable employees. In my community, former farmworkers were considered ideal employees because "you could work them to death without paying them very much," as my brother-in-law Tim loved to joke.

Few of my classmates went to college, so they had few alternatives. Some went into long-distance truck driving or agribusiness, but a number chose factory life or work in warehouses. In my community, that meant Henny Penny (a food equipment operation), Brownings (a belt warehouse), Parker Hannifin (an assembly plant), or Square D (which made electrical equipment).

But manufacturing was about to undergo its own metamorphosis. As J. D. Vance eloquently argues in his book about Middletown, Ohio, a city located just thirty miles from where I grew up, big parts of America experienced a hollowing out of its small towns through the loss of manufacturing jobs.[10] Factories long had been the mainstay of these communities because they provided good jobs for people without college degrees and allowed them to lead middle-class lives.

In the 1980s and thereafter, though, manufacturing suffered a precipitous decline. Firms shifted their operations abroad to save on labor and energy costs. A number of foreign countries featured limited government oversight, light regulation, and probusiness tax policies. From a high of 27 percent of the U.S. workforce in 1970, manufacturing jobs had dropped to 8.8 percent by 2013.[11] In small towns, there often were few employment alternatives when the factory closed.

As shutdowns spread, communities weakened and people endured considerable stress. Public services suffered because there was no tax base to support education, health care, transportation, or public safety. Hunger and poverty increased, and there were rises in suicides, alcoholism, opioid abuse, domestic violence, and child abuse.

One of my high school friends worked in a series of positions but kept getting laid off as each successive company faced hard times. In 1982, during one of America's deeper recessions, he wrote me, "I've finally found a halfway decent job after 11 months of unemployment. I'll be a sales rep for Dayton Cash Register Company. . . . McCauley's, my former employer, is about on the verge of collapse."[12] He went through the same thing in 2006. "We're on our third group of owners since I started in January 1991," he said. "There was a little job-hopping when the second owners laid off all the sales people."[13]

46

Another old friend faced new management teams as his agribusiness firm went through a series of mergers and acquisitions. In a 2006 letter, he told me, "We were bought by another big fertilizer company a few months ago. This is the sixth company I have worked for at the same location in the 21 years I have been here."[14]

Still another of my friends had severe difficulty adjusting to the economic travails. Deeply discouraged by his situation, he tried a series of jobs, but things did not work out very well and he slit his wrists. According to my sister, life was very challenging for him. She said, "He apparently had a nervous breakdown . . . a week before and had to be forcibly committed to a psychiatric hospital."

Others turned to drugs to assuage their bad feelings.[15] Referring to one of my friends, Joanne wrote me that "[his] boys are in trouble. The oldest one just got a girl pregnant. He is on drugs. His younger brother is . . . also on drugs. . . . He became so despondent he became suicidal. They had to put him in a psychiatric unit."[16]

My childhood friend Dale took solace in alcohol. He tried several jobs, from driving a truck to farming his family's acreage. But he never could escape his private demons, and he turned to hardcore drinking. At one point, he spent time in prison for threatening his sister. Even at his father's funeral, he could not stay sober. "He had been drinking before the visitation, and he also had been drinking before the funeral," wrote Joanne. "He did not go into the church where the funeral was held until the very end when only the family was up there. . . . He looked like a man who had lived hard and aged a lot as a result."[17] He died in 2013 of liver cirrhosis at the age of fifty-eight.

Alcoholism and drug abuse were no longer the scourge of large, urban areas alone. My hometown of Fairhaven, with about 100 residents on a busy day, became a drug-dealing haven for substance abusers. Outbreaks of methamphetamine and opioid abuse roiled the community. Seeing local towns destroyed by drugs and alcohol made my high school friends and relatives angry. To them, it demonstrated rural America was falling apart and America was going in the wrong direction. For comfort, many of them turned to religion. Even friends who had not been particularly religious in high school became deeply pious in the face of economic stagnation.

There even were cases of child abuse in my hometown. One of my relatives got a call from Children's Services telling her that investigators wanted to come down to discuss an incident in which a boy allegedly had touched a young girl inappropriately. For a while, the girl had been okay, but later she began having nightmares about what had been done and what might happen in the future. She entered counseling and authorities were alerted. The boy denied the allegation, but the experience divided the small-knit community. It was a town where everyone knew one another, and the accusation touched many raw nerves.[18]

At high school reunions, I could see the toll of various traumas on my classmates and their families. Most of them struggled economically, and a shocking number died prematurely. So many passed away that friends created a Facebook page entitled "Eagles Gone Too Soon" that shared obituaries documenting the latest deaths of Eaton High School graduates.

Meanwhile, my classmates could see the prosperity of coastal communities. They might not be doing well financially, but it was obvious other Americans were living it up. Those people had well-paying jobs, took expensive vacations, ate at nice restaurants, and bought waterfront properties. Their children attended elite institutions and found jobs at leading businesses, government agencies, and nonprofit associations. The contrast between the two Americas was impossible to ignore, and the ensuing anger eventually would spark a populist backlash against national elites.

Wage Stagnation and Inequality

With the collapse of agriculture and manufacturing, other sectors began to rise. There were new service jobs involving small engine repairs, home renovations, baked goods, cleaning, music teaching, or financial consulting. Digital technology spawned new positions in sales of mobile phones and home entertainment systems. This was part of the technology revolution that unfolded in many sectors.

However, many of the new jobs were based on self-employment or the use of temporary workers with no health or retirement benefits. Corporate America was learning it could downsize its permanent workforce and outsource production to independent contractors or short-term workers and avoid paying benefits. They got a hardworking labor force at a fraction of the costs of full-time employees.

The rise of new business models imposed additional hardships on midwestern communities at the very time when coastal elites were getting rich. Not only did my high school friends lose full-time factory jobs with health care benefits, retirement support, and disability insurance, they often moved into jobs that offered only episodic work, had poor benefits, or offered low pay. Gone were the days when they made good money and steadily accumulated funds to buy houses, educate their children, and take care of their families. The emergence of the new economy had many unfavorable ramifications for average workers.

For many people in the twenty-first century, economic life became more fragile and less predictable than before. As shown in figure 2-1, wages for poor and middle-income workers stagnated at the very time when incomes for high-wage positions soared.[19] For the typical worker, there was virtually no wage growth after 2000. Income data analyzed by economists Jay Shambaugh and Rylan Nunn show that "since the early 1970s, the hourly inflation-adjusted wages received by the typical worker have barely risen, growing only 0.2% per year."[20] In that situation, it was very difficult for ordinary workers to live the kind of life they wanted.

Meantime, while wages for typical wage earners stagnated, income for the ultrawealthy rose substantially. As shown in figure 2-2, the top 1 percent of earners saw their assets grow dramatically during this period. In recent years, the top 1 percent accounted for nearly 20 percent of the national pretax income (up from 8 percent in 1976)

FIGURE 2-1

Hourly Pay for High-Wage, Middle-Wage,
and Low-Wage Workers, 1979–2013

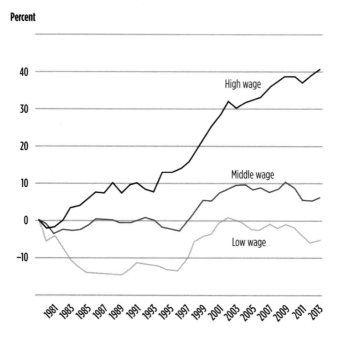

Source: Lawrence Mishel, Elise Gould, and Josh Bivens, "Stagnant Wages for Middle-Wage Workers, Declining Wages for Low-Wage Workers," Economic Policy Institute, January 6, 2015.

and controlled 40 percent of the wealth.[21] A lot of them lived on the coasts and sent their children to Ivy League schools.

Tax policies during this era fueled increases in inequality. Tax cuts went disproportionately to the rich, while the middle class saw tiny cuts that were not large enough to offset rising home prices, college tuition, and health care expenses. The rich were getting richer while the poor were getting poorer and the middle class was stagnating.

Despite this policy tilt in favor of the wealthy, my rich friends resented having to pay higher taxes during Democratic administrations. During a dinner party at the estate of one of my wealthy

FIGURE 2-2

Pretax Income Received by Top 1 Percent, 1913–2012

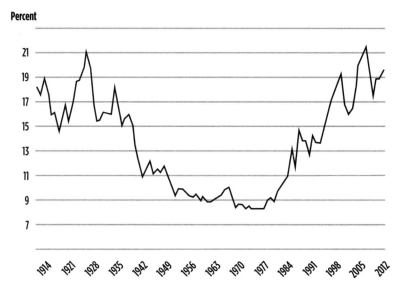

Percent

Source: Thomas Piketty and Emmanuel Saez, "Income Inequality in the United States, 1913–1998" *Quarterly Journal of Economics* 118 (February 2003), pp. 1–39. For 1999 to 2012 numbers, see the web page of Emmanuel Saez (http://emlab. berkeley.edu/users/saez).

friends, one woman complained about Obama's plan to tax the rich. Commenting on all the parties thrown by the wealthy, she suggested that "the United States should not increase taxes on the rich because all our parties create jobs!"[22] I let that justification pass but thought it was the kind of sentiment that had led to the demise of the French queen Marie Antoinette in the eighteenth century.

A Rise in Public Anger

The increasing gulf between rich and poor fueled considerable social, economic, and political tensions. With the difficult plight of the middle class in this situation, playing to the "little guy" became a potent political strategy. In 2010, unhappiness with President Obama sparked the Tea Party and led to massive Republicans gains in the House and Senate. GOP legislators blocked Obama's agenda and made it impossible for him to govern effectively. Then, in a perfect crime, they blamed Obama for not getting things done.

Six years later, Donald Trump derided bad trade deals and the loss of manufacturing jobs to other countries. He singled out illegal immigration as one of the primary reasons that native-born Americans were doing poorly. When explaining economic stagnation, he pitted whites against blacks and men against women and said experts were selling America down the river.

At a time when things are not going well, it is hard to know whom to blame. The little guy clearly is getting squeezed, and there are many theories about why that is the case. Each party has a different argument as to what is going wrong. But the uncertainty in pinpointing blame makes citizens feel powerless and suspicious regarding their political adversaries.

THREE

THE DECLINE OF OPPORTUNITY

One day at Brookings, I heard a presentation that crystallized my views about America's financial problems. My Economic Studies colleague Richard Reeves presented income data with an intriguing analysis. Based on intergenerational earning data, he showed that a person born in the bottom 20 percent of family income had only a 4 percent chance of making it into the top 20 percent.[1]

That table resonated with me because I was one of the 4 percent. My parents were poor. We didn't have much money on the farm, and we struggled to make ends meet. Through an education, though, I gained valuable skills and got a good job. That allowed me to join the professional class and make more money than I ever dreamed possible.

The current generation of Americans, however, faces a rough situation. It has been hard for them to get a good education and become economically successful. As a result, many have struggled financially and suffered poor health as a result. Most individuals from working-class backgrounds today do not have the opportunities I was offered several decades ago.

In his insightful book, *Our Kids: The American Dream in Crisis,* Harvard professor Robert Putnam describes the dramatic shift in his small Ohio hometown over the past half-century. "Port Clinton today is a place of stark class divisions, where (according to school officials) wealthy kids park BMW convertibles in the high school lot next to decrepit junkers that homeless classmates drive away each night to live in," he says.[2] Why these economic divisions have unfolded and what is needed to restore the American Dream are major sources of political conflict in the contemporary situation. People agree there is a big problem but disagree strongly regarding how to fix it.

Growing Up Poor

Both my parents grew up on small family farms. While my mother's father was working the fields, in the mid-twentieth century, she rode the draft horses. She used to operate the wheat binder, a machine that cut the crop before the grain was thrashed. When it came time to remove the wheat grain, many of their neighbors would come to help. It was a dirty job taking the grain away from their stalks, but neighbors pitched in to help one another.

My father's parents used horses to plant corn. Corn and wheat were harvested by hand, sometimes up to 100 acres of corn and 80 acres of wheat. In the mid-1940s, when Dad was in his twenties, his family purchased its first corn picker and wheat combine to harvest their crops by machine. This was a huge advance for a family that previously had relied on physical labor.

When my parents got married in 1947, Dad started farming with his father on nearby land. As the owner of the property being tilled, my grandfather took two-thirds of the profits, leaving my parents with just one-third. It was barely enough to live on, let alone support my parents' growing family.

My mother heard about a farm across the border in Ohio that was adjacent to the place where she grew up. It was owned by Jim Peterson, an economics professor at nearby Miami University. He offered farming on the halves: he and my parents would split expenses and profits. My parents saw this as a pretty good deal and left the tiny town of Liberty for the nearby community of Fairhaven, Ohio. It was only ten miles away and would be home for the rest of their lives.

Fairhaven was a tiny hamlet of around 100 residents. Established in 1832, this village was set up as a stopping point for those journeying from Richmond, Indiana, to Hamilton or Cincinnati, Ohio. State Road 177 went straight through town, and there were two churches and a large establishment known as the Bunker Hill Tavern along the main road.

In its heyday, Fairhaven was a bustling place with many shops. According to local historians, it had a general goods store, a blacksmith shop, a saddle shop, a brickyard, a doctor's office, a sawmill, a skating rink, and a roof-shingle factory. In the period before automobiles, it was a great place for stagecoaches and Conestoga wagons to stop. Four Mile Creek ran directly beside Fairhaven, and the town provided many of the amenities that travelers needed. The route through town was a popular avenue for farmers taking their sheep, hogs, and produce to the Cincinnati market.[3]

All that changed in the twentieth century. With the widespread use of cars and trucks, distances shortened and transportation speeded up, and there was no reason for anyone to stop in Fairhaven anymore. The hotel closed, and residents survived by work in nearby towns. It was one of those countless rural areas in the Midwest with few rationales for their continuing existence.

By national income standards, our family was quite poor. The average family income in 1954 was $3,960, and we were well below that figure.[4] After my parents moved to Ohio, when people asked about our house, my mother said, "There was no running water in it or hot water of any kind. No bathroom. We got things one at a time. It was the only way to do it."[5]

Water was carried in from the barn. It was not until 1952 that the house got running cold water. Indeed, because of the cows, our barn had running water before the house did. To manage the family's laundry, Mom heated water on a gas stove, washed the clothes in a manual washer, rinsed them through a hand-cranked wringer, and then took them outside to dry. There was no mechanical dryer until much later in her life. Jokingly, she said of the laundry, "You didn't do it in 15 minutes," the way she could with an automatic washer and dryer.[6]

Our first telephone was installed in 1954, right around the time I was born. The day of its arrival, my brother excitedly told his elementary school teacher, who also was one of our neighbors, there was a new object in the house. Thinking he was referring to my birth, she asked, "What is the new arrival?" Proudly, he stated, "We got a phone this week." Apparently, the telephone made a bigger impression on him than my birth.

The phone proved to be a mixed blessing, though. It improved communications and helped my family stay in touch with friends and relatives. However, to save money, we were on a party line that was shared with half a dozen of our neighbors. That gave everyone in our neighborhood the opportunity to listen in on phone calls and keep up with local gossip. This was my first exposure to community surveillance, and there were few secrets in our small town.

Tight money limited our access to medical care. My parents had no health insurance to cover my childbirth. They bore the $75 doctor's fee and $125 hospital bill themselves. My mother was fortunate to avoid complications in my breech birth delivery. These were the days before Caesarian deliveries became commonplace for these kinds of childbirths. Years later, my mother still recalled the lengthy delivery. "You were pokey. It took you hours to think about it," she joked.[7]

As a general rule, my family went to the doctor when there was a specific illness. There were no annual checkups to determine whether we might have a health problem, and preventive medicine was not a practice my parents followed. I went to a doctor a few times when I was growing up but never saw a dentist or optometrist until my teenage years.

THE DECLINE OF OPPORTUNITY

Running hot water and an indoor bathroom were added to our house in 1960, when I was six years old. This replaced the outhouse the family had used before this time. Our home got its first oil furnace in 1965. It replaced a coal stove we used in the kitchen and another in the living room. I appreciated this because my bedroom was on the unheated second floor of the house.

Despite our lack of cash, our family never felt poor because we lived in a large house and grew most of our own food. We had cows for milk, chickens for eggs, and a ready supply of beef and chicken. There was a huge garden that supplied fresh vegetables, tomatoes, berries, corn, and potatoes in the summer and canned versions in the winter.

There were twelve students in my first-grade class at Dixon, the small country school I attended. Nearly all were children of farmers or laborers. I didn't realize it at the time, but coming from a working-class background did not augur well for my long-term prospects. According to 1969 national statistics compiled by sociologists Seymour Martin Lipset and Everett Ladd, 60 percent of American academics had fathers with professional, managerial, or business backgrounds. Only 25 percent of those earning PhDs came from working-class backgrounds. And few people who receive PhDs are children of farmers.[8]

Americans like to credit individual initiative for upward mobility, but the fact is that even in an open society such as the United States, much of life success is determined by large-scale factors beyond personal control. For example, research by demographers Robert Hauser and David Featherman has found that up to 70 percent of the amount of schooling people receive is a function of family origins.[9]

In this regard, I was operating at a substantial disadvantage. Throughout the twentieth century, having a farm background was almost always a severe hindrance to future achievements. Compared with nonfarm origins, agrarian roots are highly correlated with lower educational attainment, lower family income, and higher school dropout rates.

According to the landmark James Coleman report, "Equality of Educational Opportunity," published in 1966, academic achievement depends on the quality of teachers, social composition of the school, and the student's family background. Using data from 600,000 students and teachers across the country, Coleman found that the best individual predictors of children's educational achievement were having books in the household and having parents who read to them.[10]

With their origins in small farming communities, my parents were not well educated. They never attended college, and they didn't read novels, poetry, or nonfiction. But one little-appreciated strength of many rural families, mine included, is that parents read religious stories to their children. Biblical prophets who took on the political establishment of their day (such as Egyptian pharaohs, Roman governors, or Babylonian rulers) and overcame insurmountable obstacles were prominent themes in our home. My parents never heard of James Coleman, but they satisfied two of his key findings. To further our religious instruction, they regularly read to us and infused us with optimism regarding the ability to overcome adversity.

In spring 1966, though, a health crisis rocked my world. One day, I developed a sore throat. Thinking that it was not serious, my parents did not take me to a doctor. Physicians cost money, after all, and we didn't have much excess cash. A short time thereafter, on a Sunday morning, I got out of bed and could barely stand up. My joints were inflamed and we all knew something seriously was wrong.

My parents rushed me to the doctor. In those days, you could see your family doctor on the weekend in the event of an emergency. The doctor took one look at my symptoms (a terrible sore throat, high fever, and inflamed joints) and told my parents to take me straight to the Hamilton hospital. I had developed rheumatic fever.

This was a disease that earlier in the century had been common and deadly. It afflicted those of low socioeconomic status, people without access to antibiotics, and those denied quality medical care. Caused by streptococcus bacteria, the disease generally strikes children between the ages of six and fifteen. Only 3 percent of those with untreated strep throat develop rheumatic fever, but I was one of the unlucky few.

At the turn of the twentieth century, rheumatic fever was the leading cause of death among school-age kids. As late as 1940, according to medical researcher Peter English, 2 percent of school children were infected with rheumatic fever, and a significant percentage of these died from it.[11]

But within two decades, owing to improved treatment through antibiotics, the incidence slowed to 0.05 per 1,000 population, and the death rate dropped to nearly zero.[12] After 1970, with the exception of a few isolated flare-ups, the disease was almost unknown in developed nations. In the last part of the twentieth century and into the twenty-first century, it became a disease of poor regions within Africa and Asia. In those places today, around 319,400 people die from it each year.[13]

Fairhaven wasn't exactly the developing world, but I had rheumatic fever. Fortunately, I received quick medical care that saved my life. I was in the Hamilton Hospital for two weeks. Twice a day, I received injections of penicillin. Soon the fever was under control and my joint pain gone. However, the bacterium that causes the malady attacked my heart valves. For several years after this episode, I had a heart murmur, in which one of my heart valves did not close completely and blood from the oxygenated chamber flowed back to the other side of the heart. The soft gurgling sound of backward blood flow represented what doctors called a murmur. Eventually, though, according to my doctors, I experienced a full recovery.

After graduating from high school, I was not sure what I wanted to do with my life. Like many of my classmates, I decided not to go to college. I searched for a job at local factories but had no luck. Manufacturing was starting to decline, and local factories in Richmond, Hamilton, and Middletown were not hiring new employees.

Uncertain what to do with my life, I got a job as a janitor at Miami University. It was only twenty minutes from our farm and seemed like a good way to explore what I might do with the rest of my life. I could make money and figure out a life plan. However, it took only a few weeks of cleaning toilets, emptying trash cans, and sweeping floors for me to decide to go to college.

Several years earlier, my mother had gone to work at Miami as a secretary in the political science department. The reason was that my father wanted a new John Deere 3020 tractor that cost $7,500, which was much more than our annual income. He was not happy to have her working outside the farm, but they agreed she could work a few years until they had paid off the loan.

I didn't have money to pay for college. But because my mother was a university employee, my tuition was $50 per quarter, or a total of $150 per year. Later, when I taught at Brown University, where tuition rose into the tens of thousands of dollars, I thought back to my Miami days and counted my blessings in being able to attend a great university at an inexpensive price. It clearly was the biggest bargain of my lifetime and the opportunity that made possible my professional career.

Advancement through Education

As a first-generation college student, I felt an enormous economic and cultural distance from my urban classmates at Miami. Many times during those first few weeks, I asked myself whether I had made the right decision in moving to Oxford, Ohio. National statistics showed that farm children have much higher school dropout rates than non-farm kids. I was on the verge of becoming part of that statistic.

But slowly, I started to meet people. One of the first I encountered was Laine. She was an aspiring divinity student who was not like any minister I ever had met. She smoked dope, played folk songs on her guitar, and had sex with her boyfriend. She wrote me saying, "I can't live very happily for any length of time without the physical pleasures sex affords me."[14] Unlike my childhood friends, Laine was very liberal in her political viewpoints and said that fundamentalists were narrow minded and intolerant. This shocked me because it was one of the first times anyone had told me that.

Another friend was Vicky, who had been raised in Maysville, Kentucky. She was Jewish, and we bonded as outsiders who felt alienated from our fellow students. I often discovered I had a lot in common with Jewish students, as many of them didn't feel accepted by mainstream America, nor did I. Her family was different from mine. They talked about personal feelings, and larger political and social issues. If you didn't participate in the conversations, her Dutch mother, Evelyn, pushed you to reveal your inner thoughts. No one was allowed to sit on the sidelines during those sessions.

Academically, my breakthrough came sophomore year in an urban politics class taught by Jim Woodworth. He was the chairman of the political science department, and he put a lot of creative energy into teaching. One of his pedagogic tools was a simulation he had created called Camelot. It was a role-playing exercise based on city government that had students act out the parts of mayor, city council members, business leaders, and participants in community organizations. Professor Woodworth put together a student planning group to help him run the simulation.

I became part of that group, and for the first time at Miami, I felt like a real contributor to the class. Midway through the simulation, I noticed that the student acting as mayor, a young man named Greg, was making secret decisions. I leaned over to Professor Woodworth and asked him if I could take on a role that hadn't been part of the planned simulation. I wanted to be an ordinary person in the community who was upset at secret decision making in city hall. Although this was not supposed to be part of the exercise, he agreed to my request.

During city council meetings, I badgered the mayor with criticism about how he was running the city. Why was he making secret decisions? Why was he being unresponsive to public opinion? Seeing that the public controversy was illustrating an interesting dynamic in the city, Professor Woodworth deviated from the planned conclusion of the simulation and called for an election. I announced my candidacy against the incumbent mayor. We each gave speeches about why we deserved to be mayor. Using the slogan "Win with West," I stated my belief in open government and citizen input into official decisions. In a landslide election, I trounced my opponent and was elected mayor of Camelot.

Politically, I started to move in a very different direction from my parents and became more sympathetic to the Democratic Party. I started college during the heyday of the Vietnam antiwar protests. Although I wasn't an active protester, I could see the war was going nowhere. When President Richard Nixon was accused of orchestrating a cover-up of a burglary of Democratic National Committee headquarters in Washington, D.C., the investigation and reportage by journalists such as Bob Woodward and Carl Bernstein inspired me to become a political reporter who would investigate government corruption.

My disillusionment with Nixon pushed me straight into the arms of the Democratic Party. Democrats seemed to do more to help average folks. My father used to complain that he had sent two Republican boys to Miami, and both became Democrats. This annoyed him no end, but college broadened my horizons and pushed me farther down the path of questioning my childhood assumptions.

For two summers, I had a job as a general assignment reporter at the *Richmond Palladium-Item*, a daily newspaper in Indiana. It was a wonderful job because it required me to go out into the community and interview people. I developed skills of talking to people and getting them to tell me personal thoughts for my stories. Having to put together news reports honed my skills as a writer.

However, the reporting job was pretty mundane. Rather than investigating political misdeeds, I interviewed young girls attending their first 4-H fair, covered parades and festivals, and wrote short feature articles. My fantasy of becoming an investigative reporter did not appear very realistic.

Bereft of other career ideas, I applied to graduate school in political science. It was a field that had always interested me. My brother was a political science major, and my father had become an elected township trustee. I loved politics and avidly followed current events. The field seemed to be something that would hold my interest.

I applied to a number of different graduate programs and accepted an offer of free tuition plus a living stipend from the Indiana University Political Science Department. Before I left Miami, Professor Woodworth gave me some pointed advice. He said lots of people come out of graduate school with knowledge about politics. This won't distinguish you from other people in the field, he warned. The wave of the future is statistics and computers, and that is what people need to understand. He advised me to get excellent training in statistical analysis and computer programming and predicted that these skills would help me get a job.

The Indiana department encouraged quantitative skills and did an excellent job mentoring students. PhD candidates were told to apply for grants and fellowships and publish articles. Those were the ways to get an academic teaching position at a major university. I submitted a grant application to the National Science Foundation to fund my dissertation research and was surprised when that federal agency awarded me a $9,300 grant to support my project. I also found an organization in Washington, D.C., the Brookings Institution, that provided year-long research fellowships for doctoral students to allow them to complete their dissertations. I submitted an application, and it was approved. I couldn't believe my good fortune. Now I had money and time to complete my research.

Around this period, an Indiana professor named James Kuklinski needed a research assistant for a study of voting behavior during U.S. House and Senate elections. Jim had been asked to present a paper on that topic at a Houston conference. Our analysis showed the conditions under which bad economies affected congressional contests. Citizens, we found, were most likely to vote against the president's party when they were worried about the future, and there were candidates who emphasized economic issues in the campaign. Jim wrote the paper and submitted it to the leading academic journal in the field, the *American Political Science Review*. Within a few months, it was accepted for publication and became my first academic article.

I had several interviews and received job offers from Brown University and the University of Iowa. Nearly all my advisers told me to accept the Iowa job. It was a Big Ten school and had an outstanding political science department. There were people at the university interested in the kind of work I did. Brown was an Ivy League school, but the political science department needed rebuilding. All in all, I was told, it would be better for me to stay in the Midwest.

Yet one of my advisers, Alfred Diamant, took a contrarian position. He told me there still was an Eastern Establishment and that being in the Ivy League would open doors unavailable elsewhere. Private schools had endowments that supported teaching and research, he said, and I would have more opportunities there. I took Freddie's advice and gambled on the Brown job. At the age of twenty-seven, I was going to the Ivy League. That ultimately would put me on the path to professional and financial success.

Although I didn't realize it at the time, I was starting my career at an ideal time from the standpoint of upward mobility. Years later, economists Thomas Piketty and Emmanuel Saez would document how income concentration had changed over the past century. They charted the share of pretax income earned by the top 1 percent of earners from 1913 to 2016.[15] In 1928, the year before the Great Depression, that group garnered 21.1 percent of all income in the United States. Over the next fifty years, that percentage dropped to a low of 8.3 percent in 1976, and then rose to 21.5 percent in 2007 and 19.6 percent in 2012.[16]

I graduated from college in 1976 at the most egalitarian point in American history. At that particular moment, there was a unique coincidence of progressive tax policy, government support for education, and low tuition that helped people of modest means get ahead. I had won the proverbial lottery by coming out of school at the ideal time for someone from an impoverished background.

Obstacles for the Current Generation

If I won the lottery in opportunities for upward mobility, most of today's young people have losing tickets. They face much longer odds in becoming part of the small group who move to the top of the ladder. College is much more expensive, health care costs have escalated, and the offspring of the wealthy have many advantages compared with those from working-class backgrounds.[17]

This is especially the case for those growing up in the heartland. As Reeves notes, "Rural residents often face unique barriers to opportunity compared to their urban counterparts, who can more readily take advantage of the economic activity, educational opportunities, and diversity of metropolitan areas."[18] It is harder for those in remote areas to raise themselves above their life circumstances.

Putnam makes a similar point concerning the loss of opportunity. Using his Port Clinton, Ohio, high school graduating class as an example, he discusses how the generation that came of age in the 1950s and 1960s did better than their parents, but their children face much greater challenges. For the latter group, the American Dream has slipped away and been replaced by diminishing prospects. In the current milieu, it is harder for young people to get a good education, afford quality health care, buy a house, and earn a good living.[19]

Putnam's story is similar to my experience growing up in southern Ohio. When I was coming of age, one could get an excellent education by attending public schools and universities. They had dedicated teachers and counselors who offered terrific advice. Schools were more education centers than detention homes, as often seems the case today. Contemporary teachers complain they spend much of their time on student discipline and getting young people to pay attention instead of actually educating them.

For this reason, the affluent take their children out of public institutions and send them to private schools. Most of the people with money whom I know have gone the private route. Parents pay tens of thousands of dollars a year to enroll in exclusive schools and get access to the best teachers and educational resources. The schools are safe, and students receive a great deal of personal attention. When they get into trouble or have substance abuse problems, there are counselors who provide help and make sure their lives are not derailed by youthful mistakes.

The gap between super-rich and ordinary workers has widened, and this has lowered social mobility. Disadvantaged youth suffer from outdated textbooks, rundown facilities, and counselors who have little time for individualized attention.

And the problem is not just K–12 education. Higher education is far more expensive. Figure 3-1 shows changes in the annual tuition cost of four-year colleges from 1985 to 2015. Public universities have

FIGURE 3-1

Annual Four-Year College Costs, 1985–2015

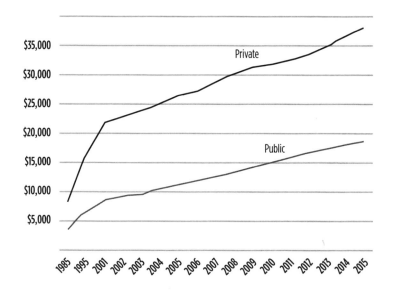

Source: U.S. Department of Education, "Tuition Costs of Colleges and Universities," National Center for Education Statistics, 2016.

gone from $3,682 to $18,632, while private universities have risen from $8,451 to $37,990.[20]

Elite private institutions charge even more. Brown University, for example, costs $53,419 in tuition and fees in 2017 plus $14,439 in room and board, for a total bill of $67,439. Many graduating seniors leave school with tens of thousands of dollars in debt that limits their options at the beginning of their careers.

Destruction of the American Dream

Recent decades have seen there has been a major change in income based on education attainment. In the 1970s, when I was coming out of college, college graduates earned about 50 percent more than high school graduates. But now, that advantage has risen to 73 percent greater earning power.[21]

America has moved toward a winner-take-all society in which top achievers do very well while others fare poorly. For the latter, the American Dream is an unattainable objective. High health care costs are part of the problem. Before the adoption of Obamacare, 18 percent of Americans lacked health insurance. That number dropped in half following passage of the Affordable Care Act, but Republicans are now dismantling the legislation and pushing more of the medical costs onto patients.

Home prices also have risen sharply in urban areas, making the costs of buying the first home beyond the reach of many young people. Even with low interest rates, many cannot afford the 10 or 20 percent down payment needed up front. Without that, they can't qualify for a mortgage and are not able to build wealth.

For those aged twenty-five to thirty-four, things have changed dramatically for the worse over the past several decades. As an example, the average debt of this demographic has risen from $10,000 in 1977 to $33,000 in 2016. The percentage who own their home has dropped from 48 to 39 percent during that time. And the number never married has skyrocketed from 20 percent in 1977 to 53 percent in 2016.[22]

Research conducted by Stanford economist Raj Chetty shows the overall impact on upward mobility. Using detailed information on family income, he found that "the share of children with higher inflation-adjusted incomes than their parents declined from around 90 percent for children born in 1940 to just 50 percent for those born in 1984."[23] As long as these patterns persist, it will be difficult to provide opportunities at the bottom or middle of the economic ladder.

FOUR

IDENTITY POLITICS

Many Americans form communities through their identification with groups based on gender, ethnicity, race, religion, politics, or personal lifestyle. This practice of sorting themselves into like-minded communities has intensified social and economic divisions and made it difficult for people to understand one another. As a result of this development, American politics has increasingly taken on the character of tribal conflict.

In her insightful book, *Political Tribes*, Yale Law professor Amy Chua worries about the antipathies generated by politically based affiliations. She writes, "The Left believes that right-wing tribalism—bigotry, racism—is tearing the country apart. The Right believes that left-wing tribalism—identity politics, political correctness—is tearing the country apart."[1]

Business executive George Eberstadt elaborates on these fears in a blog post noting the risks of this trend. He observes, "We humans are tribal animals—it is deep in our genes and our psyches. Through the evolutionary eons, those who worked together (and fought together) triumphed over those who didn't. So by its nature, tribalism is most easily and powerfully awakened in response to a threat from others: those outside the tribe. When such a threat is real, this is a healthy response."[2]

However, in an insightful analysis, he argues,

> There is a dark side to tribalism: the perception of such threats can be too easily manufactured (or grossly exaggerated) by those who stand to gain from the reaction. They say: "you must support our team! Terrible things will happen if the other team wins." Soon after, they say "in fact, the players on the other team are bad people." . . . Ironically, the fabricated threat can easily become real, as the "others" respond by organizing to defend themselves. The world becomes more and more polarized. Team loyalty becomes prized more than principle. The painstaking work of building consensus gives way to simply fighting for victory. The victors feel justified in taking the full measure of their spoils. Generosity to the other side is minimal.[3]

As someone who has spent considerable time living among the Right and the Left, I understand the concerns about tribalism run amuck. Social alignments in many American communities have fueled misunderstanding, distrust, and intolerance. There has been a fundamental breakdown in the glue that binds people together, and the negative feelings associated with those divisions have contributed to the hyperconflict that is so pervasive today.

Conservative Tribalism

When I was growing up in rural America, the tribes were mostly based on family and religious ties. People valued loyalty, and the most trustworthy associations came from bloodlines or religious values. Much of our social lives revolved around these connections.

This does not mean that family life was always peaceful. In 1907 my grandfather Walter West married my grandmother Laverne Crist over the objections of her mother. Sarah Crist feared that her daughter, who had been a sickly young child, would be exhausted by the rigors of farm life. She thought that Walter was spoiled because he was an only child. Her life plan for her daughter had been for Laverne to become a pianist and kindergarten teacher. However, in Indiana at that time, permission for a marriage to go forward was required of only one parent. In this case, my nineteen-year-old grandmother secured permission from her father, while her mother boycotted the ceremony.

My grandmother never got to teach kindergarten, but she liked to joke that she raised one. Walter and Laverne had a large family of three boys and nine girls. My grandmother used to get up at 5 a.m. to milk their ten cows by hand. As her mother had feared, Walter rarely got up before 9:30 each morning, well after the farm chores were completed.[4]

With a dozen kids, cooking, washing dishes, and making clothes were demanding tasks. She washed clothes on a washboard and hung them outside to dry. She kept three or four irons on the stove so that one was always ready to press clothes. When meals were served, she never ate with the family. Rather, she rested while everyone else dined, and then cleaned up, ate dinner, and did the dishes afterward by herself.

Walter was the disciplinarian in the family. On religious grounds, he opposed gambling with card games so there were no games of chance in his home. Although as a farmer he did physical labor, he was ill a lot. His children recalled that he required lots of rest and was frequently taking medicine.[5]

The West side of my family was more religious than my mother's side. Neither of my maternal grandparents went to church, except on special occasions. With the demands of day-to-day living, they never saw much value in organized religion or a personal relationship with God. My maternal grandfather, Harry Steele, was born in 1898.[6] He was stubborn and impatient, and both qualities got him in trouble. In 1925 he impregnated a woman named Dorothy Sheffer and was forced to marry her.[7] Not wanting the new baby (my mother) to know of the rushed engagement, they told her throughout her life they had gotten married in 1924, though the actual date was 1925. This concealed the embarrassing fact she had been born a month after the wedding.

For much of their married life, my grandparents had separate bedrooms. It was not a happy union, as the two had little in common. The strained circumstances surrounding their matrimony didn't help. There was little emotional engagement between the two, and they went their separate ways. My grandfather had a mistress and spent late nights with her. My grandmother kept records of his car mileage and wrote cryptic notes in her personal diary. One brief entry said it all: "Harry came home late again!"[8]

There was a lot of personal contentiousness on the Steele side of the family. My grandparents fought over money, particularly the meager weekly allowance Grandpa gave her. In addition, my grandfather was not on speaking terms with his sisters. That disagreement had started years earlier over the family farm. The sisters felt that their brother had not managed its finances properly and that had led to a deep estrangement among the siblings.

By the time my generation came along, my immediate family had taken on a religious tenor based on believers and nonbelievers, creating clear boundaries in social connections. The local church was the largest organizer of our personal time. My siblings and I went to church every Sunday morning and returned for youth fellowship on Sunday night. We sang Christian songs, studied the Bible, and sought to bring the personal message of Christ's salvation to our daily lives. During the week, there were Bible study sessions and other church activities. At the church we had ice cream socials and potluck dinners and attended weddings and funerals. I spent more time at the Fairhaven Church than any other place during my childhood. It was a combination church and community center and was the bedrock of our family's life.

During junior high school, I was elected president of our church's Youth Fellowship. Churches were a great way for young people to develop reading, writing, and speaking skills. There were times for organizing events, leading worship services, and undertaking analysis of the Bible. These early church experiences gave me a set of concrete skills that came in handy later in life.

For many years, I was serious about religion and genuinely thought about becoming a minister and bringing others to Jesus Christ. It seemed such an important activity, this business of saving souls. Secular jobs paled in comparison with the prospect of protecting people from eternal damnation.

As a teenager, I created church crossword puzzles based on Old Testament scriptures. These were passed out among the congregation, and people applied their knowledge of the Bible to solve word games. I remember constructing puzzles about the books of Daniel and Ezekiel, which our minister got published in a religion magazine. I loved doing these things because they allowed me to combine biblical instruction with word games.

Each week, the church bulletin listed those who were sick or dealing with some sort of stress. A prayer chain allowed those needing prayer to contact one person, who would activate a network of phone calls notifying others in the congregation. If someone was sick or had a death in the family, people brought in food. If the elderly needed someone to drive them to a doctor or the store, there always were volunteers. My closest childhood friends (Richard, Dale, Scott, and Tracy) attended our church, and we spent a lot of time socializing with one another.

In the 1940s and 1950s, midwestern country churches took a strong doctrinal stance based on the Bible. God created the world, and Jesus died on the cross to save sinful humans. All you had to do was believe in him, and you would be rewarded with eternal life. Whatever troubles you had in your human existence, such as poverty, disease, or bad fortune, would be taken away in heaven.

However, by the 1960s, the outside world began to intrude on small-town life in ways that threatened local values. For example, a group of New York parents sued a public school where their children attended complaining about a nondenominational prayer all students were required to repeat. The prayer took the following form: "Almighty God, we acknowledge our dependence upon Thee, and we beg Thy blessings upon us, our parents, our teachers and our country."

Atheists such as Madalyn Murray O'Hair seized on this prayer as an illegal violation of the U.S. Constitution. The law of the land prohibited the establishment of an official religion, and activists argued that this prayer represented a de facto effort to endorse a particular set of religious beliefs. Although lower courts ruled in favor of the prayer advocates, the legal case *Engel* v. *Vitale* went before the highest court in the land.

To the surprise of many Christians, the U.S. Supreme Court sided with opponents of school prayer in a decision issued June 25, 1962. It decreed that prayer in the public schools was unconstitutional. Teachers could not start the school day with government-sanctioned prayers. Court justices wrote that this was an unlawful infringement of the separation of church and state.

In my hometown, there was utter disbelief about this decision. How could anyone object to an invocation of God's blessings on teachers and students? Jesus Christ was not mentioned, nor was there any reference to Christian doctrines. The prayer seemed ridiculously tame by the standards of our community.

Although the Supreme Court had issued a definitive ruling on this subject, the decision did not stop my elementary school teachers from reading us Bible stories or reciting the Lord's Prayer in class. In my hometown, these were not controversial actions as there were no vocal atheists in Fairhaven. Most residents in my area believed in the Christian version of the Bible. They were not going to allow judges on the East Coast to tell them how to practice their religion.

I did not realize it at the time, but this court case was one of the most important governmental decisions in the 1960s pushing the country in a secular direction. The forces of modernity were spreading across the nation and would produce a revolution in people's thinking and behavior. Over the course of the following decades, American courts would legalize the right to an abortion, extend the rights of homosexuals and lesbians, allow schools to pass out condoms and contraceptives, and give the federal government considerable power over states and localities.

All these actions caused tremendous anger in rural America. Country folks saw officials in far-away Washington, D.C., undermining mainstream moral values and turning the United States into a secular society. For people who believed firmly in biblical teachings, these libertarian notions of personal privacy, freedom to choose, and "consenting adults" felt quite threatening.

Over time, rural churches became more militant about their fundamentalism and more insistent on the need to contest the political arena. Rather than acquiesce to what these they saw as frontal assaults on their core values, they confronted the secularism of their fellow Americans. Religious groups would stand up for what they believed and seek to roll back the forces of modernity.

In the late 1950s, our local Fairhaven Presbyterian Church hired the Reverend Don Grady as its minister. He was a charismatic and inspirational preacher who wanted to challenge the outside world and bring people to a more personal relationship with Jesus Christ. In his view, Jesus was a holy presence who cared about individual people. According to Grady, you could pray to Jesus and request guidance concerning your personal life. If you were thinking of quitting a job or making an important life choice, Jesus would let you know which option was the best one to choose. Grady told us to "pray and God's will shall become apparent to you." All you had to do was be open to his plan for your life.

At this point, both my parents became much more serious about religion. With the outside world challenging local values, they became more rigorous in their Christian beliefs. Once when I asked my mother what advice she had for me, her prescription was quite direct: "The biggest thing would be to get involved in your church.

Don't forget who our Creator is and serve him. Make him your Lord and Savior. You have to trust in him."[9]

For my brother, of course, this was a difficult option. He figured out in his twenties that he was gay and knew that the lifestyle was anathema in Fairhaven. During our youth, the restroom of the local state park just outside of town was burned down anonymously after local residents complained it had become the location for illicit gay meetings and clandestine sexual activity. There was no investigation into how it was burned down or who was responsible. It never got rebuilt, even though people regularly used the park during cookouts and social get-togethers. From the community standpoint, a state park with no bathroom was safer than one frequented by homosexuals.

In a personal history he wrote later in life, Ken described what it was like being gay in this cloistered small town. "I had no exposure to gay experiences, growing up in a conservative, Christian fundamentalist rural community. . . . I always felt different but not really knowing how or why. I guess I held back because I wasn't sure what to expect or what I wanted, or even what it was, until after I was divorced," he said.

Continuing, he noted,

I believed for many years in not coming out—I believed that self-disclosure would serve no useful purpose and also set me up for judgment by "well-meaning" but "trouble making" people. From many sources, I found that many men (and women) experienced various degrees of familial disdain and rejection, whether based on religion or concern about family image in the neighborhood. The potential for disapproval, gossip, and ridicule is an especially potent enforcer of conformity in rural, farming communities, and in the community I grew up in; families are deeply rooted and do not like to face disapproval. Today, I finally believe that being gay has been a gift from God to me.[10]

When we were growing up, I had no idea he was gay. After all, he had been married and fathered a child. But that union lasted only a few years before he and his wife split up. I still remember the time at Thanksgiving several years after his divorce when he told me he was gay. We were at my parents' home, and he was receiving regular calls from a mysterious stranger. Realizing he was in love, I finally asked him, "What is she like?" There was a long pause before he replied, "What makes you think it's a female?"

At that point, there was an even longer pause as his words sank in. I never considered the possibility that he or anyone else I knew would be gay. That option simply wasn't on my radar. As a result, it took me a while finally to stammer incredulously, "So it is a man?" Yes, he replied, and that broke the story on his romantic situation. He told me he had long felt different from other people but didn't want to acknowledge those feelings. After his marriage, though, he recognized he was gay and started to date men.

Eventually, he moved to Florida, and met the guy who would become his lifelong partner. I visited them early in their relationship, and he told me that being gay had become an all-encompassing part of their lives. They subscribed to gay newspapers, joined gay rights organizations, and patronized gay-owned businesses. During one family visit, Ken and Tom took me to a restaurant. Curious why they chose that particular place, I asked my brother and he told me that the owner "was one of us."

My mother preferred not to acknowledge the reality of her eldest son's lifestyle. Deep down, she had to know he was gay. She visited them in Florida and knew he lived with a man. The two took cruises around the world. But it was easier for her not to deal with homosexuality directly.

The only exception occurred once, in 1993, when my mother visited me in England while I was on sabbatical at Oxford University. Sitting in our living room watching *Oprah Winfrey* on British television, the segment that day happened to cover gay relationships. Although my brother had been in a gay romance for more than a decade, he had never told my mother, knowing how upset she would be. While Winfrey discussed the subject of gay people having babies, I asked her what she thought. We never really had discussed that topic before. "I don't approve of homosexuality," she said. "The Bible says people of the same sex should not lie down together."

Continuing with a comment that stunned me for its directness, she said, "I've often wondered about Ken and Tom." The two had lived together for many years, traveled together, and had purchased a home together. She said she once had asked Ken whether Tom was gay. "No" was his terse and disingenuous answer. They dropped the subject and never discussed it again.

At that point in my English living room, the conversation with my mother turned far more serious. Without looking at me, she quietly asked whether I thought they were gay. I gulped before I answered. She had never asked me that question before. After years of my brother's secrecy, I wasn't going to be the one who told her he was a homosexual. I was well aware of the adage that messengers are the ones who suffer when people don't like the news. Concealing my brother's secret, I told her, "No, I don't think so. I think Ken and Tom are just good friends."

In 2010, several years after my mother passed away, Ken called to say he and Tom were getting married in Washington, D.C., on the steps of the U.S. Supreme Court and would be sending out wedding invitations soon. Knowing that Shirley and he had never discussed his homosexuality, I asked him how he was going to inform her. "She will get the invitation at the same time as everyone else," he answered. That flabbergasted me. "You aren't going to call her up and tell her you are gay before she gets the wedding invitation to a same-sex union?" I implored. His answer was a definite no because he knew she would not approve.

I waited a few days after I got my invitation before calling Shirley. I knew it would be a difficult conversation. "Did you get Ken's invitation?" I asked. "Yes," was her quick reply. "What do you think?" I said. "I don't approve of his lifestyle and I am going to tell him that when we talk," she replied. "Being gay runs contrary to the word of God," she argued. "I love him as my brother but don't approve of what he is doing."

I waited another few weeks before I called Ken. "Did you talk to Shirley?" I asked. At that point, I felt like Henry Kissinger engaging in shuttle diplomacy between two adversaries. The two had talked, he replied, and it had been a contentious conversation. Unlike her other siblings, Shirley had never lived outside our hometown and was adamant in her thinking. As she had indicated to me, she told him she loved him but didn't approve of his lifestyle. She recently had had an operation and wouldn't be able to attend the ceremony, she said. That probably was a good decision because it would have been difficult for everyone if she and her husband had attended.

In a letter after the event, I described the wedding this way. "My sister Joanne was on good behavior. Even though she does not agree with the idea of gay marriage for religious and political reasons, she supported my brother and listened to his explanation of why gay marriage was a good thing," I wrote. Continuing, I pointed out, "If my other sister Shirley had been there, it would have been harder for her to not argue with my brother over this. She has a harder time with Ken being gay, and is more confrontational in dealing with differences."[11]

Liberal Tribalism

At Brown, there was a strong emphasis on tribalism, but the segmentation centered on gender, race, or individual lifestyle. Religion was not a very strong factor because people were highly secularized. Many students joined with others who shared their background, viewpoint, or personal experiences.

Gender was a major dividing line in university life as the school sought to address sex-based inequity and unfairness. There were numerous examples of women feeling abused or violated and believing their grievances were not being addressed by university leaders.

In 1990, for example, female students grew concerned about the university's lax policy on rape. During this time, there was growing worry on many campuses that college administrations were not taking date rape seriously. Between 1986 and 1990 at Brown, only eleven rapes were reported to campus authorities, which was thought to fall far below the number of actual assaults.

As a result, a group led by Jesselyn Brown, Jennifer David, Christin Lahiff, and Lisa Billowitz formed an organization called Brown against Sexual Assault and Harassment and argued it was time for the university to adopt stronger rules. Taking matters into their own hands, they compiled lists of "rapists, sexual assaulters, or harassers" and wrote them on bathroom walls around campus. Eventually, thirty men at Brown were labeled rapists or harassers through this informal network. Jesselyn Brown explained the action this way: "I don't think the women writing on the wall did it with the intent that it would be exposed and cause an uproar," she said. "It didn't seem premeditated. It was created out of anger and desperation."[12]

In certain respects, this effort was a precursor of the #MeToo movement that emerged in 2017. At that time, e-mail, listservs, and social media provided tools to share their experiences with prominent men who had acted inappropriately. Some women put together a spreadsheet known as the "Shitty Media Men list," which classified possible offenders under the categories of "rape, sexual harassment, coercion, unsolicited invitations to his apartment, a dude who snuck into Binders."[13] (Binders is a woman-oriented Facebook page.)

The Brown University bathroom lists sharply divided the campus. Named men complained they were falsely accused. "I have no idea why I'm there," one man wrote to the *Brown Daily Herald*. "But, hey, it's public now, I'm a rapist. They've created a whole system that found several people guilty without any recourse, without knowing who accused you. The whole justice system has been thrown out the window."[14]

Each day, school custodians would erase the lists or paint over them. The university's spokesman, Robert Reichley, condemned the wall-writers as "magic-marker terrorists."[15] Even in the days before the country's September 11, 2001, bombings, those were hot-button words. The whole episode generated so much attention that national talk-show host Phil Donahue invited the female protesters onto his popular daytime television show to explain their concerns. They repeated their justification that date rape was not taken seriously on college campuses.

As a result of this high-visibility protest, Brown toughened its disciplinary procedures and penalties for sexual infractions. In fall 1991, for the first time, sexual assault was listed in the university's student conduct code as a specific offense. Those accused would face a disciplinary board of students and faculty, which could suspend or expel guilty pupils. Those who alleged sexual assault would be referred to "advocates" who would counsel them and provide procedural advice regarding how to bring charges through the disciplinary process.

In a few years, though, the whole system would be tested in a case that generated great controversy and brought national media attention to the university. The episode began one weekend night on February 3, 1996. As reported in the *Providence Journal*, a young woman named Sara Klein drank ten shots of vodka.[16] She was in a celebratory mood because an old friend from her hometown was visiting campus. Around 11:30 that night, Adam Lack, a Brown student, walked into a friend's room at the Delta Tau fraternity looking for a compact disc. In that room, he discovered Sara lying near a pool of vomit. He claimed she talked with him and started kissing him. They had sex, smoked cigarettes, talked for several hours, and fell asleep. The next morning, Sara did not remember what had happened the night before. She asked Adam, and he said they had sex and he had used a condom.

After returning to her own room, Sara was uncertain what had transpired. "It took a while for it to actually set in. When I got home, I wasn't that upset. The more I thought about it, the more upset I got. Then I just wanted it to just go away." Her worries didn't go away. Instead, the incident lingered in her memory and continued to upset her. A month later, "I realized it wasn't going to go away. It was still bothering me, and ignoring it wasn't going to help. I guess it was that what had happened was out of control, and that I had been violated. That I had been taken advantage of and violated in a situation I had no control to do anything about."

At that point, she complained to a women's peer counselor who was assigned to her dorm. Sara was referred to a campus advocate, Mary Lou McMillan, who was director of the university's health services center. McMillan described the available options. There could be a mediation session between Sara and Adam; Sara could meet alone with a dean; she could report the crime to the Providence Police Department; or she could file a report with the university disciplinary board and request a hearing on her case.

A month and a half after the alleged incident, Sara filed an official complaint requesting a hearing in front of the university disciplinary board. On May 3, the case was heard. Responding to testimony from Sara and Adam, the group of deans, faculty members, and students found Adam guilty of "nonconsensual physical contact of a sexual nature." Adam was given a one-semester probation and required to undergo counseling on sex and alcohol abuse. In its confidential decision, the board explained its ruling by noting that Sara was impaired by alcohol and "therefore unable to consent to sexual activity" and that Adam "should have been aware of that impairment."

However, Robin Rose, dean of student life, reviewed the board's recommendation and thought its punishment was insufficient for the offense committed. She raised the penalty to a one-semester suspension and said Adam was guilty of "serious issues of personal and sexual conduct."

Although disciplinary board proceedings are supposed to remain confidential, on May 13 the *Brown Daily Herald* printed a special edition with a front-page story and picture of Adam Lack, proclaiming, "Rose Suspends Student Six Months for Sexual Assault." The newspaper story publicized an incident to an audience that previously had been known only to a small number of people on campus.

Music professor David Josephson was disturbed by how the case was handled. "It was clear to me something very peculiar had gone on and that his accuser was protected and he wasn't," he recalled. In an e-mail to the provost, the chief academic officer at the university, the professor complained that Lack was the victim of "an indecent violation of state procedures and fundamental ethics on the part of a university administrator."[17] On September 3, after his own review of the allegations, the provost reduced Lack's punishment from a suspension to a two-semester probation so he could continue as a Brown student. Lack would graduate, but several years later would die under mysterious circumstances following a neighborhood dispute near his Iowa family farm.[18]

Following the provost's decision, Professor Josephson wrote a highly inflammatory letter to the *Brown Daily Herald*. In it, he said,

> In what is only one example of the stacked deck that is Brown's student life apparatus, Lack's accuser had available to her a plethora of advisers and support systems, and finally the full weight of the student life office, while Lack had available to him only one official adviser. . . . For the past six months, he has been harassed and humiliated, his name and picture splattered on the front page of the *Herald* and on the *Herald*'s web site on the internet, his life on hold. His accuser, who remains anonymous, protected by the university, has been able to "get on with her life," unpunished for her egregious behavior; he remains under watch. The double standard to which Brown holds its male and female students, and the unequal treatment and support it grants them, has exacted a heavy toll on one young man. Brown has covered itself in shame with this farce.[19]

The letter enraged many people on campus. Critics accused Josephson of misogynist views and said the problem was that "men have become accustomed to having the upper hand." A female student wrote that the professor's "accusations of gender inequity on this campus ignore the very reason for the extensive services provided to women and minorities. That is, from the beginning of time (Adam and Eve) through the present and most likely into the future, women and minorities have been discriminated against, attacked, raped, lynched and generally kept in a level of subordination to that of white males."[20]

Similar to the bathroom wall controversy, the case did not die down. A few months later, ABC correspondent John Stossel visited campus to put together a story on the Lack-Klein case for the prime-time national television show *20/20*. Stossel was a part of the news media that loved to make fun of Brown's supposed "political correctness" and what it saw as the university's liberal hypocrisy. This date rape case fit perfectly into the external world's stereotype of Brown.

In conjunction with Stossel's visit, members of the Coalition against Sexual Assault organized a campus rally to explain their concerns about date rape. While ABC cameras recorded the scene, student speakers condemned sexual assault on campus and demanded tougher rules against sexual misconduct. The speakers argued that the time between the accusation and the hearings should be shortened, education programs on the subject should be expanded, and a confidential reporting system should be established.

After each speech making the case for tougher action, the crowd of 150 protesters chanted, "Break the silence, stop the violence" and "Rape is not TV hype." Stossel listened for a while and then asked to speak to the crowd. The correspondent explained that his network was doing a story on date rape. "If some of you want to explain to me the definition of rape—to me it's a man holding a woman at gunpoint or knifepoint. There seems to be a new way of looking at it. I'd like some of you to talk to me about it."[21]

Students were livid at his question. "We know why you came here. You knew what you were going to report before you even got here," one student shouted. According to press reports, Stossel responded with an obscenity, an amazing bit of unprofessionalism for a prominent national journalist. "Get off this campus. We don't want you here," a student yelled.

The whole scene deteriorated rapidly. "If I leer at you, is that sexual misbehavior?" Stossel asked. "Can rape be words, a look?" Later, he said, "I was taught I could do anything I wanted as long as I didn't force a woman. If a woman is drunk, it's sexual assault? Is every person supposed to be sober when they have sex? There'd be a lot less sex in America if everyone had to be sober."

When protesters objected to what he was saying, Stossel responded by thanking the protesters "for telling me what questions to ask. I'm hearing the speech police here. I'm being told what questions to ask." With student chants trying to drown him out, Stossel plaintively asked, "How about drowning us out? Is that part of the liberal Brown tradition?"[22]

The *20/20* episode aired on March 28, 1997, and was predictably hostile to Brown. The broadcast did not show Stossel's incendiary comments designed to provoke the students, but it did show the scenes of Brown students shouting him down, unplugging camera equipment, and attempting to drown out his audio. It was a completely one-sided broadcast, with students looking like they did not respect freedom of the press.

Also left out of the story, according to a friend of mine who attended the rally, was Stossel's most provocative retort. During one sparring session with a student, he asked, "Would you sleep with a woman who was drunk?" After the student indicated such an action would be wrong and contrary to Brown's code of conduct, Stossel said, "Well, I would." Students went crazy, and ABC showed their emotional reaction on the air without revealing his incendiary comment. Stossel made Brown students look completely illiberal in their political thinking.

In following years, undergraduates reinforced this negative public image when they disrupted the speeches of many prominent speakers. *New York Times* columnist Tom Friedman had a pie thrown in his face based on student discontent regarding his support of globalization.[23] Ralph Reed, a conservative strategist who had organized the Christian Coalition and helped bring scores of Republicans into office, was heckled when he gave a speech trying to address the role of religion in public life.

The same thing happened with Bush administration official Richard Perle. Speaking at a large public affairs conference organized by Brown and the *Providence Journal*, Perle was greeted with heckling about Halliburton, banging of drums, a flurry of leaflets dropped from the balcony, and unfurled banners proclaiming that he was a "war criminal." Other students painted their hands red to symbolize blood being spilled in the Iraq war.

One of the student protesters explained her group's actions, saying they wanted "to show our opinion to one of the people we're fighting against." Another justified the actions by saying "because of Perle's decisions, we, as Americans, have blood on our hands." The student described the leaflet drop as a "theatrical gesture" designed to demonstrate that "there's something fascist about this particular U.S. government."[24]

In 2001 another controversy hit the campus hard involving the issue of race. David Horowitz, a 1960s liberal turned conservative, placed an ad in the *Brown Daily Herald* entitled "Ten Reasons Why Reparations for Blacks Is a Bad Idea for Blacks and Racist, Too." Horowitz reported that 81 percent of Americans were against slavery reparations, and he claimed reparations represented a bad policy. His advertisement argued that blacks benefited from slavery, whites founded the antislavery movement, and welfare and affirmative action rules already have given blacks "trillions of dollars" in restitution.[25]

The ad came at a difficult financial time for the student newspaper. One of the reasons why the *Brown Daily Herald* had accepted the ad was that it was under severe financial pressure. A few years earlier, black students had complained about coverage in the newspaper, which at that point in time was funded largely by student activities fees. Taking advantage of the fact that student money supported the newspaper, these protesters demanded a "racial audit" of the paper's coverage and hiring practices. As a result of what it viewed as intrusion into its freedom, the newspaper refused the university subsidy of $42,000 and turned to advertising and subscriptions for revenue. When Horowitz approached it with his ad, the paper's student editors eagerly accepted his money since it would finance their operations.

The *Brown Daily Herald* ran the Horowitz ad with no explanation, no accompanying commentary, and no criticism of his reasoning. Eighteen other college newspapers had refused to print the ad. Of those that had run it, most had accompanied the advertisement with a news article or editorial commentary explaining the background on the controversial issue.

As soon as the newspaper hit the ground, the proverbial shit hit the fan on campus. The newspaper was denounced for accepting the $725 full-page ad. Black students complained that the *Brown Daily Herald* was insensitive to minorities and never covered racial issues fairly. One protester complained that for students of color on campus, "racism isn't an intellectual or academic term; it's an everyday reality." The newspaper has a history of "racially biased editorial discretion" and had become "a safe space for racist, hateful views," all justified under the principles of freedom of speech and freedom of the press.

Student protesters came up with what they thought was a brilliant public relations move. To symbolize their discontent with *Brown Daily Herald* publication of the ad and its general coverage of campus issues, they decided to remove the next issue of the paper. For students, the newspaper always has been free, and there were a number of distribution points around campus where people could pick up copies of the paper without charge. On the appointed day, there were no newspapers to be read. Shortly after they were dropped off at the usual distribution points, protesters confiscated nearly all 4,000 copies.

Nothing ticks off journalists more than outright censorship or barriers to freedom of the press. Stealing newspapers put an entirely new twist on the ad publication. Rather than debating the merits of slavery reparations and Horowitz's ad, newspapers around the country denounced Brown for stifling debate and suppressing newspapers' right to publish. Commentary pieces quickly appeared saying the university had a "viciously intolerant campus," was training a bunch of "budding brown shirts," and was "stealing newspapers for free speech."[26]

To make matters worse, the university scheduled a campus forum entitled Freedom of the Press, Community Values, Race, and Civil Discourse but closed it to the media. Again, there was a flurry of headlines denouncing the university and complaining about its close-mindedness. One journalism professor at the University of Rhode Island condemned the decision. "It's the most idiotic thing I've ever heard of," said Linda Levin. "How can you hold a forum on freedom of the press and not allow the public in?"[27] Even a local *Providence Journal* reporter, who taught a journalism class at Brown and was scheduled to participate in the forum, boycotted the event. The *Providence Phoenix*, a local alternative weekly paper with a liberal slant, named Brown number one on its annual Muzzle Awards for "repressive and censorious actions."

The university did generate some positive coverage with its strong stance scrutinizing slavery. In 2003 President Ruth Simmons, an African American woman who was a descendant of slaves, formed the Steering Committee on Slavery and Justice. Its goal was to explore the university's ties to slavery in early America and recommend actions Brown should take to atone for its unsavory past.

The university's first president, James Manning, owned and then freed a slave. Between 1709 and 1807, around 930 slave trips to Africa were financed by Rhode Island traders. These voyages brought 105,000 Africans to New England. Historical records indicate that the university's main administrative building was constructed with labor crews including slaves and that Brown had accepted contributions from businesses participating in the slave trade.[28]

The committee represented a noble effort to confront ugly aspects of the university's history. In its aspirations to deal with the past and admit historic injustices, the endeavor reflected the highest ethical pursuit. I thought it reflected a great deal of courage for the university to undertake such a full-blown self-examination.

Yet when the *New York Times* got wind of the committee, it published a front-page story saying Brown was trying to decide whether to pay reparations for its past ties to slavery.[29] Immediately, the university's development office was flooded with angry calls and letters demanding gifts not be used for reparations. Many Americans opposed the idea of reparations for slavery, and there was great intensity associated with this opposition.

Since Brown was about to launch a $1.4 billion fundraising campaign, this outpouring of opposition became a source of great anxiety for the administration. The university worried about its media image, and the front-page story in the nation's leading newspaper raised serious warning signals about this volatile topic. President Simmons issued a statement saying Brown did not intend to pay reparations for its slavery connection.

James Campbell, chair of the steering committee, denounced the press coverage. "One of the unfortunate conclusions that some have drawn from the oversimplified press coverage that we've had so far is that the committee's conclusions are somehow predetermined and, worse still, that somehow President Simmons is trying to pressure us to reach some conclusion," he complained. Neither was true, he argued.[30]

In truth, the subject was quite contentious among the various constituencies associated with the university. Students and faculty generally were liberal, but even they were divided on this subject. "Everyone in a university is always being accused of being eighteen miles to the left of the country," Campbell conceded. "But there are people on this committee who think reparations is the stupidest idea ever."

A number of parents and alumni were skeptical of reparations. At the time, families were paying around $50,000 a year for their children to attend Brown, and many did not want to see scarce resources drained off for this particular cause. At the start of a major fundraising campaign, many alumni did not believe their gifts should be used for reparations.

When the committee report came out, the university did not recommend reparations but instead focused on a variety of educational activities. A new center for the study of slavery and injustice was created, a memorial to past injustice was constructed, and new courses, lectures, and faculty dealing with these subjects were added to the curriculum. Efforts to recruit minority students from Africa and the West Indies were reinvigorated, and the university officially acknowledged its slave ties.[31]

A year later, Brown found itself in conservative crosshairs again after it expelled a fundamentalist student religious organization called Reformed University Fellowship. Arguing that the group was "possessed of a leadership culture of contempt and dishonesty that has rendered all collegial relations with my office impossible," Protestant chaplain Allen Callahan ordered the group off campus and refused to recognize it as a legitimate student organization among the twenty other religious groups on campus.[32]

Critics from coast to coast immediately condemned the action as evidence of Brown's intolerance toward conservative religious beliefs. A columnist named Richard Zeller accused the university of being a "totalitarian" state in which "anyone who takes issue with the tyrant is expelled on this basis regardless of whether the dissident or the tyrant directs the 'culture of contempt and dishonesty.'" Appearing on the Fox News television show *The O'Reilly Factor* on November 20, 2006, Greg Lukianoff, president of the Foundation for Individual Rights in Education, cited the expulsion as "another case of an evangelical Christian group getting a raw deal on campus." Continuing, he said the decision represented an example of "truly devoutly religious Christians on campus getting treated like second-class citizens."[33] A letter to the *Providence Journal* made the argument even more pointedly: "Campus sex parties are allowed but some

Christian groups may not meet on campus. I think that says it all in regard to how low this once-prestigious educational institution has sunk. It is a national disgrace."[34]

Recognizing that it was losing the public relations battle, within a week the university reversed its stance and offered a process by which the religious organization could gain reinstatement as a student group. The steps included filing a request for reinstatement and promising to communicate fully with the chaplain's office. These procedures made it easy for the group to be requalified as a student organization and use campus facilities for its meetings.

After I left Brown in 2008, there continued to be contentiousness surrounding lectures. My former colleagues at the Taubman Center set off a firestorm when they invited the New York City police commissioner Ray Kelly to speak on campus in 2013. He had instigated a controversial "stop and frisk" policy that opponents considered racist because it often was targeted on minority neighborhoods.

When Kelly arrived for the lecture, activists shouted him down and prevented him from delivering his remarks. Marion Orr, the center's director, argued that "halting a lecture is an unacceptable form of protest." Marissa Quinn, the vice president for public affairs, asked the audience to let him speak, but she too was shouted down. Afterward, she complained, "I have never seen in my 15 years at Brown the inability to have a dialogue." Outside the auditorium, protesters had signs saying "Ray(cist) Kelly" and "Don't honor the police state."[35]

The episode forced Brown's president, Christina Paxson, to write a personal letter to the entire campus saying,

> Our university is—above all else—about the free exchange of ideas. Nothing is more antithetical to that value than preventing someone from speaking and other members of the community from hearing that speech and challenging it vigorously in a robust yet civil manner. . . . Not only was Commissioner Kelly denied the right to speak, members of

our community were denied their right to challenge him. . . . Protest is welcome, but protest that infringes on the rights of others is simply unacceptable.[36]

But protesters had a far different take on the cancellation. Irene Rojas-Carroll, one of the student organizers, said, "This lecture sends a message . . . that Brown condones racial profiling." Continuing, she noted, "There is no such thing as debate between oppressor and oppressed." Another student named Rudy Torres complained, "As a person of color, I am appalled that Kelly has singled out blacks and Latinos [in his law enforcement actions]."[37]

Power Tribalism

The city of Washington, D.C., has its own culture focused on political power. Since it is located in the nation's capital, where vast sums of money ride on government decisions, the city breeds a particular kind of power-based tribalism.

My job as vice president of governance studies at Brookings gave me the opportunity to learn about D.C.'s arcane practices. One day, Henry Kissinger came to the institution to speak about foreign policy. He had served as national security adviser and secretary of state under President Richard Nixon. On the Watergate tapes, Nixon had discussed a plan to firebomb Brookings as a way to nab a copy of the Pentagon Papers thought to be stored there. The plot was never executed, but when Kissinger walked into the building, he brought smiles to people's faces by joking, "The fact Brookings still is standing represents the greatest failure of the Nixon administration."

On another occasion, I was asked to interview Fox News president Roger Ailes. He had an extraordinary business career and when he started Fox News in 1996, Fox had access to 17 million homes, MSNBC was in 22 million homes, and CNN was in 70 million homes. But by 2010, his audience had more than doubled that of the other news organizations, and the *New York Times* reported that his division earned more than $700 million in annual operating profits.[38]

I asked Ailes how he built his audience and made the business so profitable. His answer was he stayed in touch with ordinary people and understood their values. Others, however, were less charitable about his divisive emphasis on conservative "red meat." A documentary directed by Alexis Bloom, *Divide and Conquer*, highlighted Ailes's "relentless talent for pouring gas on a fire, for stoking the paranoia and fear that would keep viewers on the hook." This was a tactic his producers called "riling up the crazies."[39] Ailes understood better than most the power of nationalism and how conservatives' unhappiness with the mainstream media could allow Fox News to build a network that played to nativist viewpoints.

Taking advantage of a survey finding that 20 percent of Americans falsely believed President Obama was Muslim, I inquired what responsibility the news media have to correct false public impressions. The news executive became flustered, since Fox was a major conveyor of that misconception. He finally answered that Obama should have been more forthcoming about his Christian faith, and the onus was on the president, not the news network, to correct false views.

But the question that tripped him up the most concerned immigration reform. Based on work I had done with a nonprofit group started by New York City mayor Michael Bloomberg, I knew that Rupert Murdoch, the conservative owner of Fox News, supported comprehensive reform and had worked closely with Bloomberg on that issue. I studied past interviews with Ailes and asked the immigration question in such a way that he couldn't give a stock answer.

Seizing the moment, I inquired about illegal immigrants getting a path to citizenship and noted that Rupert Murdoch had testified in favor of that position. "Do you support that kind of pathway?" I asked. Ailes gave a long answer about the importance of border security and tough enforcement, but at the end admitted he favored a pathway to citizenship for illegal immigrants.[40]

Given all the tough Fox news coverage regarding the dangers of illegal border crossing, I was flabbergasted at his answer. If our event had been an open gathering with press coverage, that would have been the headline: "Fox News Chief Supports Pathway to Citizenship." But the forum was a private event, and no one leaked his unexpected comment. A few days later, Ailes wrote me a grateful note saying, "Thanks so much for doing a great interview with me. I appreciated the fact that you didn't point out that I had no idea what I was talking about."[41]

Of course, it was years later that Ailes was toppled at Fox after having settled a series of harassment charges from several women. It represented a shocking downfall for someone who had long been at the pinnacle of national power. But in my interaction with him, the revelations were not too surprising because it was clear he was someone not to be crossed. The reports of the power games he had played with a number of women fit his general demeanor.

In another encounter, I met Justice Stephen Breyer, of the U.S. Supreme Court, who asked Brookings to organize a get-together between key legislators and court officials. Our president, Strobe Talbott, was a friend of his and asked me to plan the dinner and panel discussion in conjunction with Breyer and staff at the House Judiciary Committee.

I went to the Supreme Court to meet with Justice Breyer in his large and ornate office across from an inner courtyard of the building. Breyer explained his hopes for legislators and judicial officials to get to know one another better. In Washington, people are so busy that it is hard to find time for ordinary encounters, whereas a relaxed setting encourages people to build relationships and form lasting bonds.

Over a series of meetings, we discussed ways to organize such a get-together, whom to invite, and what the format would be. We settled on court officials and members of the House and Senate Judiciary Committees, since those were the ones with the greatest interest in judicial affairs.

As our plans materialized, Breyer touched base with Chief Justice

John Roberts to keep him abreast of the plans. Roberts said he liked the notion of an event but then lowered the boom. Despite many months of meetings and organizational planning, Roberts asked why the Court needed Brookings to set up the dinner when it could do so on its own. From his point of view, he indicated, there was no need for any Brookings folks to be at the dinner.

That news was shocking because by that time, I had devoted hours and hours organizing the meeting and choosing participants. Most of the leg work was complete at that point, and the Chief Justice's directive was a shot across the bow.

Being relatively new to Washington power politics, I was mystified at this last-minute clampdown. But a colleague who was knowledgeable about the situation explained the likely motivation. As is common in many power circles, there was personal enmity between Roberts and Breyer, which doomed the event. Roberts was looking for a private way to embarrass his fellow justice.

A bit earlier, Roberts had announced his intention to close the main entrance to the Supreme Court and have all visitors enter the building through a basement door. According to a friend of mine, he did not want people coming in through the bronze doors under the sign that read "Equal Justice under Law." Breyer was strongly opposed to this decision and berated the Chief Justice for the closure of the route that had long led people into the Court.

Roberts waited for his moment to strike back at his colleague. In a private moment, he used the Brookings dinner event to strike against Justice Breyer. The decision barring Brookings had nothing to do with the think tank and everything to do with internal court politics. Roberts sent Breyer a stark message he was in charge and not to be trifled with over internal Court matters.

I learned another lesson about power politics when I testified in 2018 before the U.S. House Government Operations Subcommittee about the role of federal unions in the public sector. Republicans were proposing sharp curtailments in the ability of employees to use their union representatives to file grievances, deal with sexual harassment, express dissatisfaction with management changes, and negotiate with supervisors.[42]

Walking into the Capitol hearing room, I expected a hostile reception. The Government Operations Subcommittee was one of the most partisan committees in the Congress, filled with rabid conservatives. The subcommittee chair was Representative Mark Meadows of North Carolina. He had been elected in 2012 on a Tea Party platform, wanted to downsize government, had endorsed Donald Trump for president, and served as chairman of the ultraconservative Freedom Caucus. He was so conservative that he had already brought down one Republican House Speaker (John Boehner) and threatened to unseat another one (Paul Ryan) for making deals with Democrats.

For about forty-five minutes, little out of the ordinary happened. The witnesses called by Republicans explained why they thought unions served no public purpose, why labor representatives did not need official time to help their members deal with workplace problems, and how the time spent on federal grievances and sexual harassment claims was a taxpayer rip-off. I explained that sexual harassment was a big problem in the workplace, and federal employees needed help in filing grievances and resolving disputes. "Unions often are the first line of defense for those individuals," I argued.[43]

At that point, the whole tenor of the hearing changed. I had done considerable homework in preparing for the hearing, but one relevant detail had escaped my attention. In 2014 there had been allegations from several female staff members of inappropriate behavior in Congressman Meadows's office involving his chief of staff. Meadows eventually removed the man, but he continued to pay him for several months in 2015 even though his former chief no longer appeared to be working. A report from the Office of Congressional Ethics claimed Meadows had violated House rules because there was "substantial reason to believe that Representative Meadows retained an employee who did not perform duties commensurate with the compensation the employee received and certified that the compensation met applicable House standards, in violation of House rules and standards of conduct."[44]

Shortly after hearing my mention of the union role in protecting workers from sexual harassment, Congressman Meadows turned to me and said, "Mr. West, let me come directly to you because in your opening testimony, I was listening very closely." A cold chill went up my backbone because I knew I was about to become subject to a *Perry Mason*-style legal grilling.

He started with a seemingly innocuous question. "You would agree we have no idea whether official time has increased or decreased?" he asked. "That is correct," I said. "If it is a good thing, shouldn't we have more of it?" he asked. I replied that to address that premise, we would need better data on costs (which Republicans liked to emphasize) but also benefits (which GOP legislators never acknowledge). From my standpoint, there should be documentation of the positive assistance union representatives provide for their fellow workers, not just the time they take to perform those tasks.

Meadows then moved in for the frontal assault. His view was that union representatives are problematic for the federal government because they have little accountability for their time. "Those people on 100 percent official time, do you believe they have the same accountability as someone who may be on 25 percent official time to their supervisors?" he said. I responded that the statute required supervisor approval for official time, so if the boss approved the time request, there was accountability.

Not liking that answer, he shifted to an attack. "What quantifiable data do you have to back up that claim, Mr. West?" Continuing, he asked, "Do you have anything from Brookings that would prove that?" I started to say, "My sense is . . . ," but he cut me off. "I'm not asking your sense, I am asking for real data to back up your claim?"[45]

The criticisms continued for several minutes with persistent follow-ups, interruptions, and efforts to undermine my testimony. At the end, he clearly was frustrated and loudly proclaimed, "I can see this line of questioning is not producing any real results for me or Mr. West so I will yield my time."

The hearing ended and I was nervous about how things had gone. Congressman Meadows clearly was displeased with my answers. But my fears were assuaged when soon thereafter I got an e-mail from a Capitol Hill staffer proclaiming, "You were fantastic." A union official also called and said I had been phenomenal. "No one has ever faced down Congressman Meadows before," she noted. "That is the first time that ever happened." Apparently, he had a reputation for ruthlessly taking down opposing witnesses and making them wilt under critical questioning.

Still, it was shocking to hear the next day that President Trump had issued an executive order cracking down on federal unions and limiting union official time addressing workplace complaints and employee grievances to no more than 25 percent of their time. The order would end forty years of legislative support for the right of federal union representatives to help colleagues file grievances and gain whistle-blower protection.

In one fell swoop over the Memorial Day weekend, President Trump sharply curtailed the role of federal union representatives in assisting their colleagues with filing complaints and resolving workplace problems. For a president who has been the object of numerous grievance complaints and sexual harassment claims, the hypocrisy of limiting time to pursue such claims was shocking. A federal judge later would invalidate Trump's executive order on grounds that it was overly broad and ran contrary to earlier legislative decisions.

But not all public officials are personally rude. Rick Perry gained ignominy during a GOP presidential debate when he forgot the third agency he planned to eliminate from the federal government. He had been asked whether he could work with Democrats and lost his train of thought when talking about budget cutting.[46] A few years later, he came to Brookings for a personal policy briefing as he geared up for another presidential run. One of my colleagues started an answer by saying he had three points to make. Without missing a beat, Perry joked, "I generally stop at two."

Other officials were similarly friendly. One day, at Brookings, I made Senator John McCain laugh when I told him growing up on a farm had given me my lifelong goal of wanting an inside job with no heavy lifting. He was among the more down-to-earth politicians I encountered in D.C. and someone whose independence and wise judgment were sorely missed following his 2018 death.

It was technology entrepreneur Ted Leonsis, though, who taught me how D.C. truly operates. He had been one of the founders of America Online, the first internet access company. He made a considerable amount of money when AOL was bought out by Time Warner. Over the years, he had become a sports mogul and owned the Washington Capitals hockey team and the Washington Wizards basketball team, among other investments.

I had several meetings with Leonsis, talking about Brookings and why it would be great to involve him in our activities. But Ted was hard to pin down. One day, he drew on his sales background and told me about "grin-fucking"—a customer seems to encourage the sales pitch, nodding, smiling, saying nice things about your company but in the end doesn't buy the product. The grin is a façade to conceal the fact the would-be customer really is not interested in doing business with you, Leonsis explained. Based on my personal experience, what the wealthy businessman said rang true. There is a lot of grin-fucking in D.C.

Mistrusting Other Tribes

Tribal discontent reached a boiling point during the 2018 Supreme Court hearings of Brett Kavanaugh. Nominated by President Trump to replace retiring Justice Anthony Kennedy, who had been the crucial swing vote on the nine-member court, legislators of the two political parties divided sharply over Kavanaugh's legal philosophy, service during the George W. Bush presidency, and judicial temperament.

But late in the hearing process, conflict sharply escalated when Christine Blasey Ford alleged that Kavanaugh had sexually assaulted her in high school. In testifying before the Senate Judiciary Committee, Blasey Ford said an intoxicated Kavanaugh groped her, held her down, and attempted to remove her clothing without her consent in an upstairs bedroom. She recalled how he placed his hand over her mouth when she attempted to scream and laughed with his friend Mark Judge at the assault. "Indelible in the hippocampus is the laughter, the uproarious laughter between the two and having fun at my expense. . . . I was underneath one of them, while the two laughed. Two friends having a really good time with one another."[47]

In reply, Kavanaugh strongly denied the accusation. "I am innocent of this charge," he claimed, and argued that the confirmation process "has become a national disgrace." He decried the circus atmosphere and angrily interrupted senators seeking to question him. As soon as the hearing ended, President Trump tweeted his support of Kavanaugh, saying that "his testimony was powerful, honest, and riveting. Democrats' search-and-destroy strategy is disgraceful and this process has been a total sham and effort to delay, obstruct, and resist."[48]

Public opinion sharply divided along partisan lines. A CNN national survey found nearly complete polarization among the general population. Ninety-one percent of Democrats opposed the Kavanaugh confirmation, while 89 percent of Republicans supported it. There also was a strong gender gap, with women generally holding negative views about the nominee and men being more supportive.[49]

The political divide did not surprise me, as it reflected the divisions within my own immediate family. I talked to my sisters a few days after the Senate confirmed Kavanaugh on a 50-48 vote. Joanne told me she supported the court nominee. "You want to talk about polarization? I feel he is a good man who is qualified. He has been torn to shreds because of bias. It is a crying shame. . . . People are outraged in going back to high school to bring up those things. You better never have made a mistake at any point in your life."

Shirley also was upset at the Kavanaugh hearings. "The whole thing was a smear. . . . [Blasey Ford] couldn't remember anything and no one corroborated anything. It was a sham. [Democrats] have never accepted Trump. . . . Those people in D.C. are horrible. What is wrong with the people up there? They are supposed to be leading the country."

My brother and I did not share these views of the Senate decision. Ken wrote that Kavanaugh's confirmation was "deplorable. Raw power used. Disregard for women. Totally inadequate and incomplete FBI investigation." Both of us felt Blasey Ford's testimony was credible and persuasive. She clearly had suffered a lot from the high school trauma and had told people at various points about the attack before Kavanaugh was nominated for the Supreme Court. High school and college classmates submitted statements under oath that his high school drinking was often excessive and that he became angry and abusive when intoxicated. They painted a youthful portrait of the nominee substantially at odds with how Kavanaugh described himself under oath.

It is no accident the contentious nomination occurred at this point in time. During the current era, the risks of tribalism are pronounced. Technology enables people to sort themselves into like-minded groups. Social media platforms make it easy for those with strong viewpoints to find others who share their views. In day-to-day life, it might be hard for partisans to find people with similar perspectives, but on the internet, politicized communities are one click away via search engines.

In addition, the media landscape has changed dramatically. As Yochai Benkler, Robert Faris, and Hal Roberts argue, conservative outlets such as Fox News, the Daily Caller, the Breitbart News Network, and Infowars have pushed public narratives sharply to the right.[50] Conservatives have a clear perspective that has often triumphed over a disunified Left and a mainstream media that elevates political punditry over factual reporting. Even if its reporting has little factual basis, Fox News has a big megaphone and uses it to amplify key messages.

In this situation, few people trust the mainstream news media and many think reporters get things wrong. One high school friend named Carolyn wrote on my Facebook page after I did a speech analyzing President Trump's first year in office that "scrolling through social media you find a large percentage of people thoroughly disgusted with the lying, biased media. Hard core progressives are still buying the spin but for many the media has overplayed its hand."

FIVE

RELIGIOUS TENSIONS

Religion has long been a divisive issue in the United States. As James Morone points out in *Hellfire Nation: The Politics of Sin in American History*, U.S. history is filled with debates between moralists and pragmatists. In the early twentieth century, moralists won a round when the temperance movement outlawed the sale of alcohol. Prohibition did not last very long, but it showed how appeals to conservative values can have a major impact on society and politics.[1]

In recent years, new elements have transformed religious conflicts. These include the formation of community churches, political activism on the part of fundamentalists, and the rise of contentious moral issues such as abortion, evolution, and same-sex marriage. As Tara Westover vividly describes, some people with extreme views have even sought to separate themselves completely from secular society.[2]

Each of these developments has affected the role faith plays in the United States. As religious views have intensified, political conflict has sharpened and taken on a rougher hue. Believers have requested religious exemptions that absolve them from engaging in practices that are abhorrent to their faiths, such as fighting wars or making cakes for same-sex weddings. Those exemptions have increased tensions with the secular world by providing opt-out possibilities for religious objectors.

Fundamentalism

When I was growing up, I saw religious fundamentalism up close. Grandma West was a deeply religious woman. Her church was a tiny congregation a few miles from where she lived. She attended regularly and always kept a Bible near at hand. When her husband died in 1960, fourteen years before she passed away, she was confident he had gone to heaven, despite his having been a member of the Ku Klux Klan. She believed that paradise was a recreation of human life on Earth. "Families will be reunited, and husbands and wives will have eternal life together," she proclaimed. As she grew older and her own health declined, she often declared, "I am ready to go. I want to be with Dad in heaven."

Of course, if I had twelve kids and baked seven loaves of bread every day, I would long for eternal salvation too. Generations of Wests had grown up on farms holding strong religious beliefs. They went to church, studied the Bible, and prayed to God for personal guidance. Religion was not an abstraction but a guidepost for daily living. When my great-grandfather West died on the day of the signing of the World War II armistice, his widow saw one of his grandchildren and told her, "Grandpa is gone." Thinking that her grandfather was lost, the grandchild said, "We will go find him." But the child's grandmother announced the death by saying, "He's gone to Jesus."[3]

My parents were no exception, as they raised their children with the church being the fulcrum of their existence. The lesson of Noah and the Great Flood was that humans had become so evil that God decided to destroy life and start over. Because he was a God-fearing man, Noah understood divine wrath and constructed an ark that saved human and animal life. When it rained for forty days and forty nights and everything outside was destroyed, Noah's godliness was rewarded. Without his foresight, all of humanity would have been lost.

Death and destruction also featured prominently in the story of Sodom and Gomorrah, the ancient cities whose residents lived a life of sin and adultery. No one respected God, and people followed the route of carnal pleasure. In her mid-forties, my mother had learned her own father had taken a mistress to deal with his loveless marriage and had seen its traumatic effect on her mother. She took God's message about sin as a sign that humans needed to become more godly in their personal behavior.

But it was the Book of Revelation that offered the most popular missive in my local community. Its vivid description of Judgment Day, the saving of those who believed in Christ, the destruction of nonbelievers, and the Armageddon battle between good and evil were repeated endlessly in Sunday sermons. Those who do not accept Jesus Christ as their personal savior would be tormented for eternity. Hades was not depicted as a symbolic or literary illusion but an actual, physical place full of fire, sulfur, and brimstone. Snakes, dragons, and wild animals tormented those who were not saved. According to this biblical interpretation, intense physical pain would plague non-Christians forever.

At this point in my life, I feared for the salvation of my soul. I didn't know much about religion, but the worst-case scenario did not sound very promising. Eternal redemption and salvation versus eternal damnation and bodily pain? It seemed like the time for a major decision.

On March 11, 1964, when I was nine years old, I accepted Jesus Christ as my personal savior. Periodically, the church held revivals meant to bring people to Christ and renew the faith of those who might be having doubts. For four nights in a row, I heard a visiting minister explain the virtue of redemption and the long-term risks of eternal damnation. Near the end of each service, he held an "altar call": while parishioners closed their eyes and prayed to God, the minister softly intoned, "Is there anyone here who has not yet ac-

cepted Christ as their personal savior? If so, please raise your hand."
For four nights in a row, I silently raised my hand.

I felt terrible and was wracked with guilt about all the sins I had
committed. My mind raced through fights with my siblings or poor
treatment of my parents. I recalled times I had not closed my eyes
during prayer. I remembered occasions when I had doubted God's
word. I knew that on many Sunday mornings, my mind had wan-
dered from the preacher's sermon to things I preferred to be doing.

For the first three nights, I did not respond when the minister
asked those who had raised their hand to come forward to the front
of the church and pray with him. I was afraid to take this public step.
I felt embarrassed and did not want to walk to the pulpit in front of
all our neighbors and friends. Although I realized I was going to hell
if I did not make this fateful journey to the front of the church, I
could not bring myself to move my feet. I felt paralyzed by the anxiety
and embarrassment that I was experiencing. "Please let this moment
pass," I said quietly to myself, hoping these feelings of inadequacy,
torment, and uncertainty would disappear.

Finally, on the fourth night, the minister pointed out something
that was known only to the two of us, since everyone in the congregation presumably had their eyes closed during the altar call.
"Some people have been raising their hand every night but have not
accepted Jesus," he said. I knew he was referring to me. It was the
last night of the revival meeting. Fearing that I would be eternally
damned and face the physical agony of hell, I went forward that night
and publicly accepted Christ as my Lord and Savior.

It was such a relief to have made this decision. The move made
me feel like I was assured of eternal life in heaven and that I had
avoided hell's eternal damnation. A church elder gave me a copy
of the good book and inscribed it "To Darrell, on your decision for
Christ, March 11, 1964." He recommended that I memorize the sev-
enth verse of the fifth chapter of first Peter from the New Testament.
It said, "Cast all your care upon him; for he careth for you."

Looking back on this moment in my nine-year-old life, I realize my religious conversion arose more out of a fear of hell than a positive message of Christianity. Every minister I heard during the early part of my life scared me with the vivid descriptions of the fork in the road between heaven and hell. There was no middle way. Either you had eternal salvation and the glory of God in heaven or you were tormented by fire, brimstone, and serpents for all of eternity.

Ken experienced similar pangs about our religious upbringing. In his memoir, he wrote, "Church played a great role in formulating guilt feelings because our church controlled people by making them feel scared and guilty—lots of 'hell and damnation' preaching versus the love of Jesus that should have been foremost."[4]

Several years after this spiritual lodestone, a local church crisis developed that had profound consequences. A 1970 legal case brought my rural community to a major inflection point. A young black philosopher named Angela Davis became a cause célèbre in the country's liberal community when she was indicted in California for conspiracy to commit homicide and kidnapping. She was a black-power activist who was an organizer for the radical Black Panthers. A friend of hers named Jonathan Jackson had attempted to help his brother George, a member of the Soledad Three, break out of the Marin County Hall of Justice on August 7.

During the failed shootout, several individuals were killed, including Judge Harold Haley and the two Jackson brothers. When the Jackson gun that shot Haley was discovered to have been registered in Davis's name, the FBI placed her on its most wanted list. For two months, she was at large, but she eventually was captured and sent to prison.

Around the country, social justice activists accused the government of undertaking a vendetta against her. She was an avowed communist, who had been fired from a teaching job at UCLA by Governor Ronald Reagan the year before. She had been active in a number of different causes centering on race, class, and gender inequity. Friends formed a Free Angela Davis campaign to set her free. Musicians John Lennon and Yoko Ono's song "Angela" called for her acquittal.

Although the national Presbyterian Church had a number of conservative congregations around the country, the headquarters took a liberal line on issues of race and gender. In 1971, during its 183rd General Assembly, the United Presbyterian Church heard a report from its Standing Committee on Church and Race indicating that the Presbyterian Council on Church and Race had given $10,000 to the Marin County Black Defense Fund to provide legal help for Angela Davis. According to Deborah Mullen of the McCormick Theological Seminary, the reason for this assistance was "African American Presbyterians responded to Angela Davis's situation as a black woman whose right to receive a fair trial was not guaranteed in America at that time. They responded to Angela Davis as a child of God and as a black woman in racist America."[5]

When word reached Fairhaven that church money had been provided for Angela Davis's legal defense, our local congregation went into an uproar over the headquarters' support of a black communist. Both qualities put a bright bull's-eye on the Presbyterian hierarchy. As a lily-white community, Fairhaven wasn't big on interracial understanding.

Being a self-avowed communist wasn't a strong selling point in my hometown, either. Leftist philosophy might have been fashionable in liberal academic communities, but rural America had a different view of it. There was no private property in communism. Agriculture had been collectivized into giant farms owned and operated by the state. In the middle of the Cold War, local residents saw the Soviet Union as a clear military threat.

But the real crime of communism, according to my neighbors, was its atheism. Communists did not believe in God, and there was no freedom of worship in communist nations. Believers were persecuted, and Christians placed in jail. During the Cold War, ministers denounced communist leaders as anti-Christs who were evil incarnate. As forecast in the Book of Revelation, one day there would be a final battle between good and evil. An army led by an anti-Christ would sweep down from the north and confront the forces of Christianity. Following the defeat of this Satanic army, Christ would return to earth and destroy all the nonbelievers.

In my community, nearly everyone thought the Soviet Union, with its communist philosophy, was the anti-Christ nation. It represented everything that was wrong with the world. Totalitarianism was what resulted when atheism triumphed. Some even looked forward to the Armageddon battle where good would triumph over evil and the Soviet Union would be destroyed. Little did we know at the time that the Soviet Union would disintegrate a couple of decades later, but not owing to divine intervention.

Atheism made communism dangerously wrong and an outrage to be destroyed. Angela Davis was not just a foot soldier in a philosophy debate. She represented the larger battle between good and evil. My local Presbyterian church was outraged that its national council would give money for her legal defense.

Conservative congregations around the country debated what to do. My father was a member of the Fairhaven Presbyterian Church elders, the local ruling body that governed church actions. Members discussed their options, including expressing outrage over the funding decision, withholding annual dues from the national presbytery, or seceding from the national organization. The latter was a radical step because the national church owned the local church and the land it stood on. Secession meant that the congregation would have to buy back its own church.

After months of discussion, the elders in our congregation voted to secede from the Presbyterian Church. The local congregation would buy back the church and become the Fairhaven Community Church. It would be unaffiliated with any denomination and control its own destiny. Although it was not obvious at the time how important this decision would be, in later years, when abortion, evolution, and gay lifestyles mobilized conservative activists around the country, having a church freed from the strictures and controls of the national body gave local congregations the ability to act as they wanted. They could recruit ministers, spend money without oversight, and operate according to whatever doctrine they desired.

In time, local community churches across rural America became much more politically active. Freed of national bureaucratic oversight, churches could follow their own religious and political paths. Liberal church organizers on the East Coast no longer could tell local midwestern congregations what to do and what values to follow.

Community-based churches adopted stances in keeping with local values, not liberal viewpoints common on the East Coast. Congregations would become much more active and eventually would help conservative politicians win control of the American national government. They would elect a string of conservative politicians from Richard Nixon and Ronald Reagan to George H. W. Bush, George W. Bush, and Donald Trump.

Years later, I was walking across Brown's campus and spied a university flyer advertising a speech by Angela Davis as part of Black History Month. I recalled the enormous impact she had on my tiny Ohio hamlet and that people in our congregation thought of her as the anti-Christ. At Brown, of course, having a radical leftist speak on campus was not a divisive issue. I went to her lecture, which was attended by more than 600 people.[6] She gave an impassioned speech that people in my hometown would have hated. "The protocol of racism I learned as a child I no longer have to observe today," she noted. "But I would be grossly exaggerating the contemporary circumstances of the city if I generalized by saying we have successfully eliminated racism."

But this was not Fairhaven, Ohio. In the Ivy League, her message was well received, and most people agreed with her critique of America as a racist society. Almost all the people I knew walked out of that lecture praising her commentary on the prevalence of racial injustice in America. Faculty colleagues and students saw her as a courageous beacon shining a spotlight on societal unfairness.

Secularization

As an adult, my religious views shifted more in a secular direction. When I moved to the East Coast to teach at Brown I was still engaged with religion, but not in a fundamentalist way. I read new discoveries about historic texts, and what I learned about early Christianity surprised me. In 1945 Egyptian peasants discovered a large cache of "forbidden" gospels, including the Gospels of Thomas, Philip, and Truth that were excised from Christian orthodoxy. Called the Nag Hammadi Library, this set of fifty texts shed new light on the origins of early Christianity and how Christ's apostles disagreed on major points.[7]

In addition, between 1947 and 1956 more than 800 different Old Testament scrolls were found in eleven caves along the Dead Sea, thirteen miles east of Jerusalem. Known as the Dead Sea Scrolls, these manuscript discoveries date back to the period between 200 BC and AD 68, and reveal how religious beliefs unfolded during that crucial time period.[8]

Taken together, these manuscripts demonstrated the impossibility of taking the Bible as literal truth. As pointed out by biblical scholar Bart Ehrman of the University of North Carolina, the newly discovered writings revealed how the early church was sharply divided about Jesus's divinity. Some early Christian congregations felt Jesus was the son of God, while others promoted him as a wise prophet who provided new understanding to guide human beings. There were disagreements as to whether Christ represented a reform branch within Judaism or a whole new way of relating to God. Others were uncertain whether Christians should believe in a single deity or a spiritual trinity based on God, Jesus, and the Holy Ghost.[9]

According to historical discoveries, Jesus was crucified around AD 33. In AD 70 the Romans destroyed the Jewish temple in Jerusalem to put down a major rebellion. It was a time of great persecution in Israel. The suffering and despair led the followers of Christ to write down his sayings, as many were looking for spiritual guidance during this period of great strife. Over the period from 70 to 100, the gospels were transcribed and letters to churches in Corinth, Ephesus, Rome, and Thessalonica from the Apostle Paul were written down.

The new writings discovered in the twentieth century reveal an early church of competing factions, divided by ideology and plagued by bitter disputes between various groups of believers. There was no orthodoxy among early Christians, and the process by which church doctrines were decided unfolded generations after the death of Christ.

Two centuries after the death of Christ, church leaders agreed twenty-six books should form the New Testament. Other books that were widely read by Christians over the first two centuries were suppressed on grounds they did not fit into the mainstream view. Those rejects were burned, discarded, and forgotten until being found 2,000 years later.[10]

Bart Ehrman, who started life as a fundamentalist, explains that the current version of Christian doctrine won

> because [its promoters] were better debaters. Each of these groups was fighting all the other groups on various fronts, but the proto-orthodox seems to have been better organized than the other groups and to have been more intent on establishing a worldwide network of similar people. And so they ended up taking over the churches in the major areas where there were lots of Christians, such as Rome, and eventually in Alexandria, Egypt, and Jerusalem.[11]

It took generations after Christ's death for church leaders to coalesce around views that are now considered tenets of Christian practice: Christians should worship on Sunday, Christianity was distinct from Judaism, Christ was the son of God and part of a divine Trinity, and Christmas would be celebrated on December 25 and Easter in April. None of these conclusions were widely accepted until religious leaders grew tired of the endless debates, dictated key points of church dogma, and exiled dissident leaders and books who espoused other viewpoints.

None of these discoveries, however, helped me resolve doctrinal disagreements with my sisters. They accepted a literal interpretation of the Bible. After seeing a dramatized play about the Book of Revelation at a Cincinnati theater, Shirley wrote, "I have been praying for you every day for a long time that something may stir inside your heart so that you may believe in Jesus Christ. I grow more and more concerned every day because I believe the end times are getting close at hand." Continuing, she noted, "when Christ comes, it will be too late for anyone who hasn't accepted Christ. There's no second chance after he comes, they will be cast into the lake of fire. I just needed to tell you this myself because I care and I don't want it to be too late for you."[12]

Around that same time, Joanne told me about dark forces in America. "We feel Satan is really moving in and succeeding in making people get away from God. . . . We see how Satan is working to make things keep going down."[13] For her, the devil was a real force who fought with Jehovah for the hearts of people. It was not an abstract debate, but one with direct personal consequences.

I was not surprised at these sentiments because they were the viewpoints that had dominated our upbringing. For years, I had struggled with the reconciliation of a fundamentalist youth and secular adulthood. Describing this tension, I wrote to my minister friend Laine and said, "My world has been different from theirs for a long time, but it is becoming more different all the time. It makes the transition hard for me because we share so few of the same assumptions, like about religion, morality, and politics."[14]

In a situation of factional fighting and sharply contending beliefs in the early church, it was hard for me to see how literal interpretations of the Bible could remain convincing to modern-day Christians. Views common among contemporary fundamentalists—that the

Bible is the direct word of God, that there is one Christian view, and that the Good Book is the literal truth, are contradicted by historical evidence demonstrating extensive diversity in early Christianity.

Even the original apostles, who were Christ's closest followers, did not agree on the meaning of their faith. Saints Peter and Paul had different conceptions of Jesus. Paul, in fact, never met Jesus because he converted after Christ's crucifixion and had to rely on second-hand sources for his knowledge.[15]

When Karin and I visited Israel a decade ago, we gained a deeper appreciation of the intensity of religious beliefs. We visited the sites most holy to Jews, Muslims, and Christians: the Wailing Wall, the Dome of the Rock, and the Church of the Holy Sepulchre.[16] We started at the Wailing Wall, the most sacred spot for Jews. It is the large western wall that used to form the base of the Jewish Temple destroyed first by King Nebuchadnezzar of Babylon and then by the Romans in AD 70. It consists of large, carved stones piled on top of one another. Jews come to the wall to pray, and the site had great meaning for them because of its ties to King Solomon's original temple.

We then went to the Temple Mount, where the Dome of the Rock is located, the holiest site for Muslims. It is the place where the Prophet Muhammad is said to have mounted his horse to fly to heaven. The mount is a huge flat concrete area that can accommo-date large crowds of visitors. The Dome is a Muslim mosque with a beautiful gold dome and blue and green tile covering the exterior. It makes for a spectacular sight in the bright sunlight. However, non-Muslims are not allowed inside the mosque. My wife was wearing an open cut blouse and the guard at the entrance of the Temple Mount asked her to put on her shawl to cover her bare neckline.

After lunch, we found the street Via Dolorosa and followed the path Jesus Christ had taken from his sentencing by Pontius Pilate to his crucifixion site, now marked by the Church of the Holy Sepul-chre. There are fourteen stations on the walk marking various events along Christ's final sojourn. This includes the place where Pilate sentenced Christ (now the courtyard of the Umariyah School), the Franciscan Church of the Condemnation, where Christ received his cross and crown of thorns, and spots where Christ fell, saw his mother, and spoke to Jerusalem women.

Within the Holy Sepulchre Church are the places where Christ was crucified, taken down from the cross, and buried. The sepulchre or burial site includes the rock that guarded the entrance to Christ's tomb. It is housed in a big wooden structure. Inside the tomb are two rooms. The outer room is large and has a picture of Christ. Then, you must lower yourself under a three-foot-high doorway to enter the interior room. It is very small and has space for only a few people at a time. It is designed to be intimate and personal for each individual. There is a picture of Christ and a marble tablet covering the spot where Christ was laid out. There are candles and ornate objects surrounding the gravesite.

The crucifixion chapel marks the spot known as Golgotha, where Christ was believed to have been crucified. Within the chapel is a glass structure with a marble tablet having a hole in the top. If you reach down inside that hole, there is a stone believed to be the stone on which Christ's cross was placed. A marble tablet just outside the crucifixion chapel is thought to be the place where Christ was laid to rest following his death on the cross. Pilgrims come here and fling themselves on this plate as a sign of respect for Jesus.

The visit to these three spiritual centers helped me understand my own religious past and the differences between Jews, Muslims, and Christians. Many members of each faith view their religion as the only true perspective and feature adherents who will fight to the death for their beliefs. But as new historical evidence comes to light, it becomes hard to maintain fundamentalist interpretations of any faith.[17]

A contemporary joke explains our modern dilemma regarding doctrinal purity. Several people of different faiths go to heaven and are met at the pearly gates by a saint. As they are ushered down a hall, the saint cautions them to be silent as they float past room 106.

Once they are safely down the hallway, the saint tells them it is okay to rejoice. "Why do we have to be quiet at room 106?" one of the souls inquires. "Oh, that's where we put the fundamentalists," the saint replies. "They think they are the only ones up here."

By the time I came to Rhode Island to start my job at Brown University, I felt a spiritual void that led me to resume my search for religious community. The best thing about small-town religion is that people care about one another and look after those who are having problems. No one is anonymous; every person counts for something.

What pushed me back to the church was an unthinkable tragedy in 1991. A friend of mine named Alice Brendel was murdered, along with her husband Ernie and young daughter Emily. It was one of the most horrendous crimes ever to befall the state of Rhode Island.[18]

I had met Alice shortly after my arrival at Brown a decade earlier because she was the government documents librarian at the university's Rockefeller Library. My first administrative assignment at Brown was being the political science department's library representative. Through that position, I encountered Alice and enjoyed her keen sense of humor. She was soft-spoken but very competent and well-respected in the university community.

One day she did not show up for work. Concerned people went to her house in Barrington, a beautiful suburban community south of Providence located on Narragansett Bay. There was no sign of Alice, Ernie, or Emily. For weeks, everyone waited for a break in the case. None of the Brendels appeared, and there were no signs of their bodies. Police searched area woods, rivers, and dumps, all to no avail.

Seven weeks later, there was a break in the case. Police discovered that a man named Christopher Hightower had handled financial investments for Ernie, and the two had fallen out over a commodities deal that turned sour. The relationship had grown so strained that Ernie had reported Hightower to the authorities over an alleged impropriety in the man's business practices.

In what turned out to be one of the state's most notorious crimes, Hightower had shot Ernie with a crossbow and strangled Alice as an act of revenge. It was never clear how Emily died, but investigators speculated the eight-year-old might have been buried alive underneath her mother. Deranged by the soured business deal, Hightower had killed the entire family and hidden them in unmarked graves.

Alice was a member of Central Congregational Church in Providence. This church sat in the middle of the upscale East Side just a few blocks from the Brown University campus. It had several hundred members and one of the most beautiful domed sanctuaries in the area.

Following her murder, the church held a memorial service for grieving family members, friends, and co-workers. As a friend, I attended the ceremony and was impressed with the dynamic minister, Rebecca Spencer, who conducted the service. Rebecca was the first female minister of that congregation, and I immediately liked her. She came across as smart, thoughtful, and caring.

As I looked around the church that day, I felt a genuine sense of community. The congregation offered Bible study groups, book reading clubs, women's groups, men's groups, youth groups, and bike-riding activities. Regardless of one's interests, there were people with whom you could share a spiritual or emotional bond.

Its bulletin featured inclusive language on gender and proclaimed, "We affirm that all of us are created in God's image, regardless of age, gender, race, ethnicity, sexual orientation, mental facility, economic circumstance, or physical condition." Gays, minorities, and people of all backgrounds were welcome. There was little rhetoric about fire and brimstone and no apocalyptic sermons about eternal damnation of your soul.

In her sermons, Rebecca called for tolerance and understanding of one another. She supported the view of Learned Hand that "true wisdom is the spirit of never being totally sure you are right," a very nonfundamentalist perspective. On another occasion, she proclaimed, "There are no bouncers in the Church of Christ. Everyone is welcome." The church served as a meeting place for Alcoholics Anonymous and it took collections for poor people who were hungry or those who had suffered personal misfortune. There were groups for individuals who had lost loved ones and needed spiritual guidance.

This East Coast church represented a stark contrast to the evangelical approach prevalent throughout midwestern and southern congregations. In the decades since I left Ohio, Protestant churches had become quite militant about expressing their political viewpoints. Ministers preach openly about social issues of the day. They argue Western civilization is in decline, and it is time to take a stand against secular humanists.

In 2005, grassroots organizations sympathetic to these perspectives joined with Reverend James Kennedy of Coral Ridge Ministries to organize a Reclaiming America for Christ conference. Kennedy told participants that "our job is to reclaim America for Christ, whatever the cost. As the vice regents of God, we are to exercise godly dominion and influence over our neighborhoods, our schools, our government, our literature and arts, our sports arenas, our entertainment media, our news media, our scientific endeavors—in short, over every aspect and institution of human society."[19]

These statements were not idle talk. Before Election Day, ministers told parishioners to make sure their electoral decision reflected the values of God. Preachers generally did not have to say more because members of their flock understood the message: Vote Republican and stop the country's slide toward sin and moral depravity.

In some fundamentalist communities, parishioners went even further. Conservative activists used church lists to mobilize members on Election Day. Cars outside the church on Sunday morning were leafleted with antiabortion literature. Phone banks would rely on church directories to spread the word about conservative candidates. This was a fight for the heart and soul of America, and it was important for believers to act on their faith.[20]

I could see the influence of the conservative religious movement through the activities of my nieces Laura and Katie and nephews Mark, Doug, and Jeff (my other niece, Amy, grew up in Florida, outside the range of my hometown's religious fervor). Like me, they were pressured to become born again. Joanne described the night it happened with Mark. She wrote, "Tim and I took the youth fellowship to a play in Richmond depicting the judgment seat after you die and then seeing the glory of going to heaven or the terror of being dragged off to hell kicking and screaming. Twelve kids went. Mark Mitchell went forward [to accept Christ]. . . . Mark had tears in his eyes and his lips were quivering."[21]

These and similar experiences were meant to solidify training that would last the rest of their lives. When Katie started dating a divorced man, Mark told her this behavior ran contrary to biblical dictates. He e-mailed her several verses he claimed proved his point and, when she continued the relationship, informed her she "didn't get good spiritual advice."

Jeff took a chastity vow and promised not to kiss or touch a woman until he got married. Even when he met an attractive young woman named Katie, he kept this promise. He went out with her for over a year and never kissed her. The first time they kissed was after he asked her to marry him and she agreed to do so.[22]

Laura's husband, Doug, attended men's religious gatherings known as Promise Keepers. These conferences combined study of religion, relationships, and family life and attempted to teach men to be good husbands. This surely is a noble activity that many men need. But Promise Keepers has a very traditional approach to family life in which men are supposed to be in charge. Laura and Doug signed a "marriage covenant," which they hung over their bed. Doug promised to take care of Laura, and Laura promised to submit to Doug.

Several of these relatives attended religious universities or undertook "mission trips" to spread the word of Jesus, some organized under the auspices of the Campus Crusade for Christ. This group organizes sets of kids on each college campus and teaches them how to raise money for missionary activities and prepare for these excursions.

My nephews took mission trips to exotic locales around the world. Mark went to Baku, Azerbaijan, for a year. One of the former Soviet republics nestled on the Caspian Sea between Russia and Iran, Baku was 93 percent Muslim. Jeff went to England and Russia on mission trips. Doug went to Ocean City, Delaware, to convert U.S. nonbelievers.

In each of the locales, Campus Crusade for Christ taught kids how to blend in, meet people, and offer services that would become a vehicle to bring people to Jesus Christ. In foreign countries, one of the favorite approaches was teaching English classes. The missionaries would go to places where young people hung out and introduce themselves to the locals. If the person expressed any interest in talking, the missionary would invite the person to an office where English was taught or social activities were organized by the group.

As their friendship developed, the missionary would ask about feelings of loneliness or distress. When the young native invariably confessed to these thoughts, the missionary would indicate he too felt that way but had found that the love of Jesus conquered those ill feelings. Over time, more and more religion would be brought into the conversation until one day, the missionary would ask the person to convert to Christianity and accept Jesus Christ as his or her personal Lord and Savior.

After he came back from Azerbaijan, Mark wrote that "through the course of the summer, the 21 of us got the chance to share with hundreds of students and it was really encouraging to see the fruit of 23 Azeris convert to Christianity!! Personally, I got the opportunity to see a student named ____ make the decision to follow Christ! He struggled with the decision for about 2 weeks, and when he decided to become a Christian, he took the Koran (the Muslim holy book) off from around his neck and gave it to me, saying that he didn't need it anymore!"[23]

Continuing, Mark told me how important this mission had been to his spiritual journey. "This trip was definitely a life-changing experience for me spiritually and personally," he said. "Throughout the summer I have come to the realization of not only being a Christian and knowing what I believe, but I also know exactly why I believe what I do. I also know that I am looking for a genuine relationship with Jesus, not just knowing that He saved me, but truly wanting to know Him personally, and involving Him in every aspect of my life!"

The most impressive thing about devout fundamentalist Christians is their ironclad belief in the value of each human soul. Many secular humanists are daunted by social change because unless they can see big results from their activities, they doubt their effectiveness. Fundamentalists, on the other hand, consider themselves successful if they save one soul. Every individual has value, and if you are able to save one person from eternal damnation, you have achieved a major success.[24]

Jeff was very proud when one of his hometown neighbors accepted Christ on his deathbed. He had done odd jobs for the man, and Joanne described the end-of-life scene: "A week ago Jeff approached him, and Charlie was not receptive. He was last night, and Jeff cried the whole time he prayed with him. What an awesome experience. Jeff told him he wanted to see him again. Jeff told me he asked him to tell Grandpa [West] hi!!"[25]

Doug Atkins had the same experience when his father fell ill. After being diagnosed with stage IV cancer of the esophagus, lymph nodes, small intestines, lungs, and liver, his father stopped treatment and went into a hospice. While there, according to Shirley, "his dad made a transformation from saying he had peace with God, to really understanding that Jesus died for him and he accepted Christ on his deathbed. Doug was so much at peace (and so was his mom) in knowing he would now one day see his father again in heaven."[26]

The religious issue personally came to a head for me one day in 2005 when my mother encountered a major health problem. She had been mowing her lawn on a hot day at our Ohio farm when she felt dizzy. Hoping it was a passing symptom, she kept mowing. However, when her eyesight started to blur, she shut off the mower and called my sister. After a trip to the emergency ward, the doctor informed my mom she was suffering from low blood sugar. She was diabetic and if she did not eat enough, her sugar level dropped to a dangerous level. He sent her home with instructions to take it easy and eat proper food.

Two days later, she suffered a debilitating stroke that left her paralyzed on one side of her body. She could not move her leg or her arm
and her speech was quite slurred. For a few weeks, she struggled to
regain her health. Her speech slowly came back but the left part of
her body remained paralyzed. Having a stroke always had been my
mother's greatest fear. She had seen her own mother paralyzed in
bed following a stroke. My mother had taken care of her, but never
wanted to subject her children to the same imposition.

When it became clear she would not regain use of her limbs, my
mother quit eating and slowly faded away. It was clear her wish was
not to linger. It took several weeks for her system to shut down, and
at 7:10 a.m. on July 1, 2005, with me by her side, my mother stopped
breathing and quietly passed away. She never wanted to be depen-
dent on others and was at peace with her family.

Following her funeral, my sisters told me my mother had left
some advice for each of her children. For her two daughters, she said,
"Keep the music flowing." They both were pianists, but the advice
was broader than music. Over the years, my sisters had disagreed
over many issues. In 2007 Joanne had written an angry e-mail to
Shirley that warned "sometimes I feel like you would be so much
better off if you didn't even have me as a sister. Then you wouldn't
have to always be making judgments about me or second guessing
my decisions or my availability or anything."[27] They had remained in
our small Ohio community and lived just ten miles apart, but prox-
imity had not been good for them. Although they agreed on politics,
they had different perspectives on child rearing, church matters, and
family relationships. They should keep the peace and stop fighting,
my mother implored.

For my brother and me, her final advice was "I hope they accept
Jesus into their hearts." This reflected her wish that Ken and I become
more fundamentalist in our religious practices. Ironically, her words
echoed advice my father gave us in 1985, two years before he passed
away. In a taped reminiscence about his life, he had told us, "I pray
my kids and grandkids also accept the Lord as their Savior and know

what life is all about."[28] Although our parents knew each of us was spiritual, neither thought we were very serious about religion. Both of them wanted their sons to have a personal relationship with Christ that would guide our daily decisions.

Religious Exemptions

In recent years, new fault lines have opened over religious issues. The separation of church and state is firmly established in the United States. Following a number of court cases, justices have ruled that authorities cannot impose religious values on those who do not share those viewpoints. For example, Christians cannot impose their principles on Jews or Muslims. That includes school prayer, Bible reading, and religious displays such as nativity scenes.

But within that framework have grown a number of legal exceptions, and many current religious conflicts concern these exemptions.[29] In 1990 Justice Antonin Scalia wrote a majority opinion in the *Employment Division* v. *Smith* case, ruling that the United States is one nation and all Americans are required to respect its laws. The issue in this case concerned whether there should be a legal exemption carved out for Native American tribe members who wanted to smoke peyote on religious grounds. In Scalia's opinion, the answer was no. According to the ruling, the state of Oregon was justified in firing the perpetrators and denying them unemployment benefits.[30]

In the past few years, though, there have been successful efforts to carve out exceptions on religious liberty grounds. As an illustration, when the Obama administration passed the Affordable Care Act, it required employers to provided mandatory access to contraceptives. Its reasoning was that contraception was important for health care and employers should make it available to every worker who wanted it. This was very much in keeping with the prochoice orientation of women's rights organizations and major currents within society at large.

Managers at the Hobby Lobby chain, however, sued on grounds

that this was an unconstitutional infringement on its legal rights. According to its lawsuit, the U.S. government cannot establish a religion and impose its values on other people who don't share those views. That would infringe on religious liberty and violate the establishment clause of the Constitution.

The *Burwell* v. *Hobby Lobby* case went before the Supreme Court in 2014, and justices decided on a 5-4 vote that the Hobby Lobby Corporation had legal rights and the Affordable Care Act imposed an unfair burden on it. The case established a religious exemption that allowed companies that did not wish to comply with the contraception requirement to opt out and not provide birth control for its workers.

A similar exemption request came up in regard to same-sex marriage. A Colorado baker named Jack Phillips, at Masterpiece Cakeshop, objected to homosexuality on religious grounds and refused to sell a wedding cake to a same-sex couple, Charlie Craig and David Mullins. Craig and Mullins sued, and the case went before the Supreme Court. On a 7-2 vote, the Court ruled on narrow grounds that the same-sex couple did not have a right to purchase a cake from a baker who expressed religious objections to the homosexual lifestyle.[31]

Joanne was surprised that a major Supreme Court decision had gone in favor of Christians because in her view, most court cases over several decades had been won by secularists. When I asked her reaction to the ruling, she said, "The way things have been going in recent years, I think it could have gone the other way. Under Obama, it wouldn't have gone this way. He had no tolerance for anyone's faith."[32] Continuing, she expressed sorrow for Jack Phillips and complained he had lost his business in defending his right to refuse service to homosexuals.

Yet other religious people complained their fellow Christians didn't lift a finger when President Trump separated immigrant mothers from their children in a border crackdown. A Rhode Island minister named Sharon wrote on Facebook that "for some Christians, baking a cake for a gay wedding is against your Christian faith and principles, but watching children taken and jailed with no information or hope of being reunited is okay with you? I think we all need to put down Leviticus and try the Gospels."[33]

The legal case shows how the longtime battle between believers and nonbelievers has morphed onto new terrain. Believers lost the battle to practice their beliefs in official settings, but they are winning the fight for legal exemptions to certain laws. Under certain compelling circumstances, believers have leeway, according to the courts: citizens should not be subject to a law that constrains them from the exercise of their religious beliefs.

An example from North Carolina shows how this is happening. A civil magistrate objected to same-sex marriages on religious grounds. She worked out an exception in which she did not work during times of the day when weddings took place. However, the state rejected that accommodation, and she was forced to resign to protect her religious beliefs. Citing court rulings, a federal judge overturned that state policy, though, and said she should have been allowed to alter her work schedule to avoid having to officiate at same-sex weddings.

The magistrate wrote a newspaper column praising that court decision. She noted, "Our civil rights laws—and many Supreme Court cases—encourage employers to do lots of things in the workplace to ensure that people of all backgrounds are valued, respected employees. Individuals with disabilities are given special equipment. Muslim workers can obtain scheduling accommodations for prayer breaks or dress-code deviations for headscarves. Government workers have been excused from handing out fliers for meat products because they were vegan. Prison guards who disagree with the death penalty are allowed to avoid being involved in executions."[34]

Those loopholes, however, show how religious disputes have seeped back into public life. Conflicts over moral principles now result in a situation where particular laws are not enforceable on all individuals. If the person can demonstrate a compelling religious reason, he or she can refuse actions that compromise those principles. That creates legal exemptions that widen the gap between people of divergent lifestyles.

In that situation, the potential for misunderstanding or outright intolerance is quite high. Someone who seeks an exemption from a law believes he or she is doing this for principled reasons, while those who do not receive a service available to others almost certainly feel bias or discrimination on the part of the individual withholding service. This is just one more way contemporary decisions have heightened societal conflict.

As a sign of the widening schism over religion, my brother sent me a humorous meme: Obama complains, "Trump's reversing all of my policies," to which Jesus responds, "The evangelicals are reversing all of mine."[35] This was not a joke my Ohio relatives and friends would have found very funny.

SIX

THE BACKLASH AGAINST GLOBALIZATION AND IMMIGRATION

Disagreements over the U.S. relationship with the rest of the world are among the conflicts that have emerged in recent years. Several decades ago, America embarked on a globalization strategy that expanded trading relationships. The hope was that free trade and more open immigration policies would stimulate economic growth, promote cross-cultural understanding, and improve the lives of many people.

That strategy, however, has created a backlash over unfair trade deals, foreign terrorism, and the possibility of lost jobs. The movement toward a globalized world has stalled and been superseded, at least in part, by a climate of nationalist sentiments and xenophobic fears. The traditional left-right divide has morphed into disagreement about whether we want a more closed or a more open relationship with the world.

Opening Borders

When communism fell in the early 1990s, the United States saw an opportunity to remake the global landscape. Rather than continue a Cold War with adversaries around the globe, the country shifted to a globalization strategy that would expand markets and encourage the flow of people, goods, and services across national boundaries.

Trading was seen as more likely to generate positive results than hostile relationships. The assumption was that increased commerce and border flows would improve prosperity and knit the world closer together. If people from different lands dealt with one another and had cross-cultural ties, it was thought, international tensions would be reduced and nations would constructively connect with one another.

Passage of the North American Free Trade Act in 1993 represented the first step in this direction. The act created a free market with no tariffs between the United States, Canada, and Mexico. Businesses could move products across national borders and trade freely with one another. This was followed by other pacts. China was admitted to the World Trade Organization in 2001 and became a large trading partner of the United States. There were agreements with a number of other countries to decrease tariffs and improve commerce.

In addition, immigration was seen as good for the United States. President Reagan signed a historic immigration reform bill in 1986 that provided amnesty for those in the country and created a pathway to citizenship. As our economy developed in recent decades, immigrants filled jobs that native-born Americans no longer wanted to perform.[1] This included positions staffing hotels and restaurants and working on farms.

The latter task, of course, I understood completely. Most Americans do not want to engage in physical farm labor because of the dirt, heat, and cold. Even decades after my own agriculture experience, I still can recall how difficult the job was and how exhausted I felt at the end of each day. Immigrants' willingness to perform farm and other kinds of work is a huge benefit to the agrarian and service economies.

For this and other reasons, I am generally sympathetic to globalization. International experiences have enriched my life and given me a greater understanding of other cultures. Meeting people from different backgrounds and learning about their societies has helped me understand that people in various countries share common aspirations.

My first overseas trip came in 1987 to Berlin, Germany. My wife, Annie, had an international botanical conference there, so we decided to piggyback family travel on top of that trip. I remember flying into Berlin and realizing how much history had unfolded in that locale. Germany was at the center of both twentieth-century world wars, and this divided city now was on the front line of the Cold War between the Soviet Union and the United States.

A high concrete wall separated the East from the West, and armed guards patrolled the no-man's-land in between. I wanted to see the wall and spend a day in communist-controlled East Berlin. My mother begged me not to go, fearing that communists would kidnap me and never let me go.

It was an eye-opening adventure to cross the border into East Berlin, see the guard towers, and visit stores with bare shelves. Many stores were open but bereft of retail items. The food products for sale did not look very appetizing by American standards.

Two decades later, I had the thrill of returning to Berlin and seeing the reunited city. The ground where a concrete wall once stood had grown new buildings and pedestrian walkways. The city was upbeat, alive, and united under one government. Germany seemed to be a place where opening borders had paid off.

By that time, I already had seen what happened to another country (Japan) that had closed itself off. In 1990, the year I visited there, Japan was at the beginning of an extraordinary economic collapse. Its real estate bubble burst, and the nation went into a financial depression that lasted more than two decades. Unemployment grew, interest rates dropped to zero, and there was no economic growth for a prolonged time.

There were many reasons for the fall of Japan, but being a closed society and hostile to immigration were major parts of the problem. Japan was a homogeneous society that provided few opportunities for women, minorities, or foreigners. It intentionally kept immigrants out, even though this limited its population growth and economic development. With a stagnant population and an aging workforce, the country did not adapt well to an innovation-based world.

In addition, the young people there were not encouraged to think independently. On a bullet train to Kyoto, we met a young Japanese college student from Hiroshima who shocked me by asking if I had ever heard of his city. Understanding his reference was to the use of nuclear bombs in World War II, I assured him Americans knew his hometown and had not forgotten its nuclear bombing.

We had a very engaging conversation about many aspects of Japanese society. He asked us what we did and when we told him we were college professors, the tenor of the entire conversation changed. Although he was sitting in a train seat, he bowed deeply, and his earlier friendliness gave way to a stiff formality that was not nearly as revealing. He was so constrained by social hierarchy that he no longer could speak freely with us. It was distressing to see such a change in the tenor of the conversation.

Cross-Cultural Tensions

The 9/11 terrorist attacks in the United States provoked widespread fear regarding threats from outside our national boundaries. The hope that globalization would bring greater peace, prosperity, and international understanding seemed either naïve or completely wrong. In response to the attack, a number of American leaders called for tighter scrutiny of foreigners, tougher border controls, and more guarded engagement with the world.

I could understand this change in sentiments, especially in the

American hinterland. People there weren't seeing many benefits from globalization. All they saw was movement of manufacturing jobs to Mexico, China, Vietnam, and the Philippines. From their standpoint, globalization was an empty promise with few benefits for them.

In my travels to the Middle East, I experienced firsthand the rise of cross-cultural tensions. Many countries there weren't benefiting from increased trade, and the resulting lack of prosperity was harming their social, economic, and political fabric. Owing to improvements in global communications, their residents could see other countries doing well and wondered why they were not sharing in the prosperity.

One such place was a 2002 visit to Lebanon. It was the scene of a bloody civil war based on religion, social class, and ethnicity and a country with a very difficult history. There had been a number of wars at various points in time, and the nation had been overrun by foreign forces. It was a place that had difficulty controlling its own destiny.

While visiting there, I met a young woman who worked for the Lebanese Ministry of Finance. She was thirty-four and had grown up right on the infamous Green Line that divides Muslim from Christian areas and served as the battlefront for much of the civil war. She explained that she went to school throughout the conflict but was not able to venture out much other than going to classes. To distract her and give her something to do, her parents taught her and her brother a variety of skills such as knitting and embroidering.[2]

Despite these efforts, she said, the war imposed a psychological toll on everyone. People became focused on themselves and worried about all aspects of their personal safety. It was difficult to form relationships, and occasionally she still had gunfire flashbacks in her neighborhood. It amazed me that people could live through that kind of trauma and maintain some semblance of normalcy.

I had another conversation with a twenty-three-year-old Lebanese woman, who had grown up in a coastal city just north of Beirut.

Her father had been very strict with her when she was growing up. Following Middle East customs, he insisted she not go out by herself. Her mother and close friends, though, helped her evade these strict rules. Mother and daughter would say they were going out together to the same place. When they arrived there, the mother (or friend) would go elsewhere, and this woman would spend time with her boyfriend. When she was done, she would call her mother on a cellphone (which her father didn't know she had); the two would rendezvous and go home as if they had been together the entire time. Such is the deception that Middle Eastern women are forced to practice because of the strict rules required by their male relatives.[3]

My trip to Lebanon helped me understand why the various religions in this region have difficulty coexisting. Each faith there is quite demanding of its adherents and very expressive in dealing with the community. For example, every night in Beirut, people gather in mosques for evening prayers and worship. However, the mosques are not content merely to house worshipers inside their sanctuary; the leaders insist on large amplifiers that carry the sounds throughout the city. No one practices the faith quietly.

The Middle East is one of the most fascinating places in the world because modernity coexists side by side with feudalism. A trip to Bahrain showed how autocrats persist alongside modern skyscrapers and sophisticated technology. Bahrain is a small island country in the Persian Gulf just off the coast of Saudi Arabia. Until 1986, no bridge linked the two countries. That year, though, a causeway bridge was built, and it was a boon to travel and trade between the two countries.

Saudi Arabia is a strict Islamic regime that allows no alcohol, music, or dancing. However, on weekends, many Saudis drive over the causeway to Bahrain to partake of drinking, women, and entertainment. Local residents are amused at the hypocrisy of their Saudi neighbors, who love to do things there that are forbidden at home.

Bahrain itself is a throwback to the world of centuries ago. It is ruled by a monarch and its local newspaper features stories citing local fundamentalists who believe artistic performances run contrary to Islam. Rather than fighting these beliefs, government authorities have shut down some public performances.

One day there, I had a strange encounter with a Muslim couple in a hotel elevator. My room was on the eleventh floor, and I was going down to the lobby. I was in the corner of the elevator when it stopped at the tenth floor. At first, I didn't see anyone, but then a woman dressed completely in black walked into the elevator. Her face was veiled except for a narrow slit for her eyes. She was startled when she saw me, as was her husband, who was accompanying her. They whispered something to each other and then pressed the button for floor nine. They rode down one floor and got off. As the door closed, I heard them push the button to call another elevator. Perhaps they had forgotten something and needed to go back up to the tenth floor. But judging from their clear discomfort, it appeared likely that they called another elevator because they didn't want to ride down to the lobby with an infidel.[4]

Tough Enforcement

It isn't just Arabic citizens who are suspicious of foreigners; many Americans have developed the same mentality. I learned this the hard way after I met Karin, who would become my second wife, and witnessed her passage through the American citizenship process. She worked for the U.S. State Department in Munich and was the consulate public affairs person who arranged lectures, conferences, and seminars.

Karin had been raised in a small Bavarian town of a few thousand inhabitants about eighty miles north of Munich. Her father, Hans, served in the German army, while her mother, Christa, worked around the house. Christa had lived in the contested Sudetenland between Germany and Czechoslovakia; she migrated to Bavaria in 1945 after Germans were expelled.

We had both grown up in rural areas and had to deal with communities that were conservative in politics and religion. Karin loved discussing human psychology, religion, politics, and German-American relations. We stayed in touch, and eventually married.

As a foreigner living in America, Karin brought a fresh eye to my native land. When the Boston Red Sox won the World Series in 2007, she asked the innocent question why Americans called this a world series when only U.S. baseball teams participated in the play-offs. She did not buy my answer that it was because American teams had internationalized with players from Japan, Cuba, and the Dominican Republic.

Other times, the cross-cultural gap produced funny exchanges. When I took her to a local bank to open a checking account, the young bank clerk got confused when the front of her passport listed her native origins as "Deutschland." He wanted to know what country that was. I had to explain to Karin that geography was not a strong suit for many Americans.

Like most Europeans, Karin loved to ride her bike. It was a great way to get around town. However, she quickly discovered the car culture that dominated American cities. Riding her bike one day down an East Side street in Providence, she was shocked when a driver leaned out his car window and yelled, "Hey, lady, get a car!" She resisted the impulse to yell back at him, "Hey, guy, get a bike!"

But our biggest U.S. adventure concerned the immigration process. As a native-born resident, I had no idea until I married Karin how difficult it was to become a citizen. I assumed marriage automatically made her a citizen and that administrative approval would be simple and straightforward.[5]

It therefore was a surprise when the U.S. Citizenship and Immigration Services rejected her citizenship application on grounds we weren't actually married. We had been married for five years at that point and assumed sending the agency a copy of the marriage license along with other bits of evidence would document our union. With this highly bureaucratic organization, though, the marriage certificate proved only that we were married on the date of the ceremony, not several years thereafter.

None of my academic or professional credentials prepared me for the rigors of dealing with the immigration office. The encounter was exhausting and perplexing but helped me understand changing U.S. attitudes toward foreigners. Despite our Statue of Liberty welcoming the huddled masses, in reality, America no longer sees immigrants as an unmitigated good.

Getting a green card and becoming a citizen is very expensive. Citizenship and Immigration Services is funded by applicant fees, not federal tax dollars. That means it is expensive, perpetually under-staffed. There were charges for taking fingerprints, fees for filing each form, and then another cost if you filed the wrong form.

As part of the green-card application, my wife signed away her right to basic government services. She would not be eligible for public assistance as long as I had assets to support her. I had to list my salary, savings deposits, personal property, stocks, bonds, and life insurance policy demonstrating that I had income at least 125 per-cent of federal poverty guidelines so that she would not become a "public charge" of the United States.

In Providence, Rhode Island, where we initiated the green-card process, and in Washington, D.C., where my wife applied for citizen-ship, the offices for collecting biometrics were in distant suburban communities with no bus lines or mass transit. This was not a prob-lem for us since we owned a car, but without it, the constant trips would have been a nightmare.

For many immigrants, it is virtually impossible to afford the fees, handle the paperwork, and navigate a complex bureaucratic process. My PhD in political science did not prepare me for the complexity of the multiple applications, fees, documentation, interviews, and trips to the immigration office.

Transportation and money aside, though, that was only a whis-per of what loomed ahead of us. There were many obstacles along the path to citizenship. The immigration office has an open distaste for technologies that are a staple of American innovation. All the government immigration forms are paper and require hours of photocopying important documents to accompany the forms (sometimes more than once when they invariably get lost). Materials could not be electronically transmitted to immigration authorities, despite the lost opportunity to save money, avoid lost documents, and speed up the process. Virtually every communication involved physically going to the post office or mailing documents back and forth.

The most shocking decision came with our citizenship application. We filed forms showing we were married, but the application was rejected on grounds we hadn't proved our marriage was genuine. The agency had a fortress mentality that assumed one is lying unless one can definitively prove otherwise. Friends suggested we send pictures of our honeymoon, but they didn't realize such images would prove little in the eyes of immigration authorities. For clearer evidence, I put together documents including tax returns, bank statements, insurance forms, employment status, and even Facebook pages showing we had gotten married in 2007 and been living together on a continuing basis since that time. Trips out of the country had to be documented to show that our periodic absences from one another were not evidence of a sham marriage.

In April 2012, we went to the D.C. immigration office located an hour outside of town. We were ushered into a small room with a hearing officer. She had our thick stack of documents in front of her. We feared the worst, but she gave us good news. She said our file looked good and we would get a letter confirming Karin's citizenship application.

We were ecstatic that our appeal seemingly had worked. But as the old saying goes, never spike the ball until you are in the end zone. We waited for months to get the official letter, but nothing arrived. I wrote a memo noting the positive hearing and requesting clarification of her case but got no response.

I e-mailed the agency using a new electronic communication address it had set up, but there was no response. I called the agency's 800 number, and the person who answered informed me his computer was down and consequently he could provide no help. When

I called back, I got another person who said the last thing in our online file was the citizenship denial. There was no record that our April appeal even had taken place. On another occasion, an immigration officer asked Karin to retake the citizenship knowledge test of American history, even though she had passed it months earlier with a perfect score.

Eventually, one immigration phone operator gave us a very helpful hint. "Go to the immigration website," he advised, "and request an in-person meeting." The volume of letters and e-mails the office receives is so heavy there often is no response. Throughout November and December, I went to the agency's InfoPass website to request an appointment, only to get a message every time saying no appointments were available. Around Christmas, I got lucky. We received a January 11, 2013, appointment for a meeting at the local office.

The day arrived, and we made the early-morning drive to Fairfax. We met a pleasant young man in his twenties and explained that Karin's citizenship request had been denied in December 2011, and that we had had an April 2012 hearing but had gotten no communication over the past half year. He looked at his computer and said he would go to a back room to check our file. Ten minutes went by and I worried about worst-case scenarios.

After a long wait, the young man reappeared with a supervisor. "Good news," he said. "Your citizenship application actually was approved last April following your hearing." Among the various scenarios I had role-played in my head, this was not one I had expected. "Our application was approved six months ago?" I asked incredulously. "Yes," he said. "Did you send us a letter informing us of this?" I inquired. "No, we didn't," he replied sheepishly.

The news slowly dawned on us. My wife's application had been approved months earlier, but no one had called, written, or e-mailed the approval. Instead of delivering the good news, the agency had demanded new fingerprints, a new citizenship test, and a new hearing. Each part of the agency has no idea what other sections are doing. Even with multiple phone calls concerning our case disposition, no one had informed us our documents were in order and she had been approved. It was a mind-boggling conclusion to a five-year process.

I wrote up the story of what had happened in a Brookings blog post and sent it to a number of people. Carnegie Corporation president Vartan Gregorian, himself an immigrant, wrote a nice note saying, "Thank you for sharing your Kafka-esque tale of the path to citizenship for your wife. It certainly brings home the dysfunction of the immigration system and the need for reform. Congratulations on making it through to the end."[6]

A few weeks later, Karin was sworn in with more than 100 other immigrants at the federal courthouse in downtown D.C. It was a joyous occasion filled with great emotion for everyone in the room. More than fifty countries were represented, and the new arrivals were proud to become Americans. Many were crying and sharing warm embraces with family members. But the forbidding and intransigent bureaucracy we had endured was a sign of how America was turning against new arrivals.

Ultranationalism

Following the Great Recession of 2008–09, Americans openly rebelled against both immigration and globalization. They saw jobs migrating out of the country, American businesses relying on part-time workers with no benefits, and far less job security for the average citizen. All that made them angry about the failed promises of peace and prosperity. A number of people felt they had been sold a bill of goods by U.S. leaders.

After I wrote a Brookings article describing European efforts to "reeducate" terrorists so they would become law-abiding people, my friend Linda sent me a scathing response reflective of the new mood:

I had no idea education of radicals is being done in Europe. Typical liberal thinking to be tolerant and try to reason with radicals via education to make them be nice to everyone and quit cutting off heads and making bombs. It reminds me how the current government is controlling the education in this country, trying to get the youth accustomed to be controlled, giving them free stuff, promoting socialist ideas. Not likely to be successful fast enough to stop killings, any more than you'll ever convince me to vote democrat.

It is quite obvious the problems and killings that are going on in Europe when these refugees are brought into the country. And yet chronic lying Hillary wants to bring the same shit here. What kind of logical reasoning is that? She seems to think maybe if she invites them to tea, they won't want to kill her. And the gays are dumb enough to think Hillary is the answer if they want to keep their gay rights. Even after seeing gay night clubs are a big target for these radicals to hit. Re-education is fine as a long term goal, but in the meantime, these radical camel fucking nut cases need to be put on an isolated island by themselves. We can show compassion by dropping some survival equipment and food off to them, and let some liberal do gooders who are willing to get killed run the re-education camps, but trying to get them to go from one extreme and assimilate, without a lot of us getting killed, is pure stupidity. We need protection from these fuckers.[7]

Linda was not the only one who felt this way. Politicians came along to capitalize on these reactions and popularize a more inward-looking message based on border protection and ultranationalism. Trump argued that America was under attack and being sold out by businesses that shipped jobs overseas. He said the country should build a wall along the Mexican border to keep out illegal immigrants who brought crime, violence, and disease to the United States.

After he became president, Trump set about delivering on his promises. He signed a travel ban barring immigration from several predominantly Muslim countries that ultimately was upheld by the Supreme Court. He claimed those individuals were terrorist risks and therefore should not be allowed in where they might endanger ordinary Americans.

As he had promised during the campaign, President Trump also moved to curtail legal immigration on grounds those individuals were taking jobs from native-born Americans and eliminated legal protections given by President Obama to the "Dreamers," young children who had entered the United States illegally with their parents. His view was that open borders had exposed the country to unnecessary problems for the economy and national security.

At the same time, Trump cozied up to strongmen around the world. He praised rulers such as Vladimir Putin of Russia, Recep Tayyip Erdogan of Turkey, Xi Jinping of China, Abdel Fattah el-Sisi of Egypt, Mohammad Bin Salman of Saudi Arabia, and Rodrigo Duterte of the Philippines. Commentator Stewart Patrick of the Council on Foreign Relations warned, "The issue is a troubling one. Trump's lionizing of the 'strong' leadership qualities of authoritarian personalities like Putin, Erdogan, Duterte, and Sisi—as well as his own attacks on free press at home—cannot help but embolden their efforts to crack down on civil society and crush dissent in their own countries."[8]

At a technology conference in Moscow, I saw Putin's authoritarianism up close. When major U.S. figures enter an auditorium, they smile, shake hands, sign autographs, and pose for pictures. But when Putin came to the event to deliver a speech, there was no effort to curry favor with attendees. Without any announcement, he entered the room ten feet from where I was seated, strutted down the aisle, and went up on stage without any smiles, hellos, handshakes, or pictures. He immediately started his speech, talked for fifteen minutes, and left without speaking to anyone. It was a rather remarkable display of arrogance, and it was clear he didn't care a bit about people.

Many of Trump's foreign and domestic moves sharply divided America. If political conflict had seemed intense under earlier presidents, Trump raised it to new heights. Conservatives in the Midwest and elsewhere shared Trump's antipathy to illegal immigrants and saw them as criminals and security risks. But liberals saw the chief executive as a clear and present danger.

Even innocuous comments on Facebook set off my progressive friends. When I posted a picture of President Trump's three helicopters departing D.C., they replied in full snark: "devil's triangle" (Jay), "if only he were truly gone" (Kim), and "please don't come back" (Bob). Only one friend defended Trump with the exhortation to "hurry back" (Johnny).

Numerous people in my network hated Trump's actions against immigrants. They thought immigrants helped the United States by filling jobs in agriculture, hotels, and restaurants that most Americans did not want and adding new flavor to American culture. Most migrants brought their local food, music, and perspectives to the United States and therefore enriched the entire nation.

A Twitter acquaintance named Andrew wrote of the following encounter at a gas station. "A guy comes up after seeing my "FUCK TRUMP" sign. Him: You know why we love Trump so much? Me: No. Him: Because he gets under the skin of liberal faggots like you. We don't care what he fucks up, as long as he pisses you off," he said.[9]

A Rhode Island friend named Stephen meanwhile liked the fact that Trump stuck to his views on major issues. He wrote on Facebook, "I had to put up with Obama for eight years. That wasn't easy as he broke from so many traditional American values. . . . I've grown to like the prez because he keeps his word."[10]

Underlying much of this debate, though, was a deeper argument about what it means to be an American. Experts predict that because of immigration and differential birth rates among various parts of the population that sometime around 2045 white Americans are likely to lose their majority status.[11]

The reason for the sharp drop in the white population is a combination of low birthrates, immigration, and high mortality rates. Non-Hispanic white women have fewer babies, on average, than Latino women. At the same time, 82 percent of the immigration is coming from Central America, Latin America, or Asia. Moreover, much of the white cohort is at the upper end of life expectancy.[12]

Figure 6-1 charts how dramatic this change is. In 1950 about 90 percent of the country was non-Hispanic white. This dropped to 69 percent in 2000 and is projected to decrease to around 60 percent by 2020, 49.9 percent in 2045, and 43.6 percent by 2060.[13] This was an outcome that many older, white Americans did not support as they wanted the country to stay the way it had been, not turn into a multiracial polyglot.

There is a major partisan divide in how Americans view these demographic trends. A Public Religion Research Institute survey re-

FIGURE 6-1

Non-Hispanic White Share of U.S. Population, 1950–2060

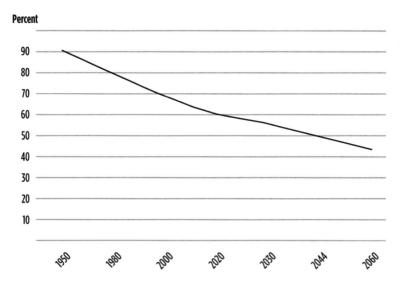

Source: Data from Michael Walsh, "U.S. Percentage of Non-Hispanic Whites Hits All-Time Low of 63%," *New York Daily News*, June 13, 2013; Sandra Colby and Jennifer Ortman, "Projections of the Size and Composition of the U.S. Population: 2014–2060," Bureau of the Census, March 3, 2015.

vealed that 85 percent of Democrats think rising diversity is "mostly positive," compared with just 43 percent of Republicans. According to Brookings scholar William Galston, religion and education are major determinants of these differences. Only 42 percent of white evangelical Protestants and 50 percent of whites without college degrees are favorable to demographic diversity.[14]

Race and ethnicity are undercurrents of many contemporary divisions. For example, following neo-Nazi violence in Charlottesville that killed an innocent bystander, President Trump equated the violence of white supremacists with that of the minority community. That argument played well with the president's white base, yet minorities and progressives were appalled. They felt Trump was stoking racial resentment and using "dog whistles" to divide people from one another.

In 2018 an AP-NORC poll found that 57 percent of adults "think Trump is racist." Equally alarming, 57 percent believe his policies have been bad for Muslims, 56 percent say they have been bad for Hispanics, and 47 percent feel they have been bad for African Americans.[15] Many Americans told the pollster that race relations were getting worse and that the president's comments proclaiming African countries "shitholes" contributed to the discord.

The president's immigration policies sharply elevated the emotional stakes of the national debate. One *New York Times* commentator wrote a provocative column, entitled "Trump Wants to Make America White Again," alleging that "the aggressive pace of deportations of immigrants of color, the elimination of the DACA program protecting immigrant children and the proposals propounded by the anti-immigration voices in the administration will all have the undeniable effect of slowing the rapid racial diversification of the United States population."[16]

The fight over borders is no longer a disagreement over immigration or globalization but is rather a far more fundamental battle regarding the demographic future of the country. What should America look like, and how is the country going to handle the shifting relationship between women, minorities, and the older, white men who occupy top positions in business and government? It is a highly contentious debate that is not easily resolved by conventional politicians. This battle represents one of the reasons nearly half of the country was willing to turn to someone like Trump, who does not accept common assumptions or act in typical ways. His supporters feel that extraordinary times call for extraordinary leaders and not politics as usual.

Two years into his presidency, Shirley continued to express her strong support of President Trump. She attended one of his rallies outside of Cincinnati in the lead-up to the 2018 midterm elections. When I asked for her reaction, she wrote me, "It was exciting to be there! President Trump did a wonderful job! The crowd was very enthusiastic, which made it very exciting! In fact, when the president came, it was a roar!!! When he spoke, the crowd responded enthusiastically. It was just so exciting to be a part of it! I'm so glad I went! It was a wonderful chance to see the sitting President of the United States!"[17]

SEVEN

UNDUE INFLUENCE

Perceptions of special interest influence have made many ordinary Americans feel the current system is rigged against them. These individuals know they have not fared well economically while the top 1 percent has seen its wealth grow exponentially. That discrepancy has fueled populist beliefs that the average person is not well served by contemporary leaders.

Based on my experiences, there are a number of ways in which the system has tilted against typical folks through outright corruption, the college admissions process, and philanthropy. These developments have fueled public sentiments that powerful leaders have disproportionate influence and insiders benefit unfairly from the overall system.

Overt Corruption

My first experience with corruption came early in life when my father bribed a milk inspector to get a clean bill of health for our family's dairy operation. This particular inspector had been making my father miserable by complaining that our milking equipment was dirty and we were not in compliance with food safety standards. Visiting one day, the inspector casually mentioned that he had a small flock of chickens and it was hard to get corn to feed them. "We have lots of corn," my father informed the inspector. "Why don't I give you a few bags?" The inspector accepted the gift and for the first time in years, our dairy operation received an exemplary cleanliness rating.

When I moved to Rhode Island in 1982, I discovered much more widespread misbehavior. It was a machine state where Democrats controlled the General Assembly, town councils, and many of the statewide offices. Ever since the 1930s, when national Republicans had failed abysmally to deal with the devastation of the Great Depression, Rhode Island had voted Democratic. It had all the classic features of a one-party state: patronage politics, personalistic disputes, and endemic corruption. Politicians fought for every advantage they could get. Johnston Mayor Ralph Russo even changed his last name to aRusso, in order to be listed first on his city's alphabetically defined ballot.

Unlike larger states where the politics are more anonymous, Rhode Island featured what my political science colleagues Elmer Cornwell and Jay Goodman called the "politics of intimacy."[1] When former U.S. House Speaker Tip O'Neill proclaimed that "all politics are local," he must have had Rhode Island, as well as his home state of Massachusetts in mind, as everything in both states was local and personal.

Shortly after I arrived in Rhode Island, the state elected a Republican governor named Ed DiPrete. The Cranston mayor had campaigned as a reformer who would clean up politics from the mess of the Democratic machine. It was a fascinating change for a place used to Democratic dominance. DiPrete said all the right things about wanting to reform the state and bring efficiency to the public sector.

But soon, there was an action that would question these intentions. In 1988 Governor DiPrete and one of his sons took a hometown property they had purchased, won a favorable zoning rule that allowed for property development, and sold it a short time later for a $400,000 profit.

It was a shocking use of inside contacts to make a huge profit. DiPrete looked just like an old-style politician who was enriching himself and using personal connections for private gain. Publicly, I became critical of him, and several years later, I felt vindicated when the governor pled guilty to extorting hundreds of thousands of dollars in bribes.[2]

By the subsequent election, the state's economy had tanked, the real estate boom had crashed, and business failures were increasing. Governor DiPrete's approval rating dropped to 16 percent in public opinion polling, and one local magazine joked that if he stayed in office much longer, it would hit zero.

Governor DiPrete was tiring of my criticisms and media predictions of his political demise. On October 5, 1990, a month before the general election, the state GOP leader, John Holmes, had lunch with me at the Capital Grille, a prominent restaurant near the state capitol. Holmes was friendly and talkative. He discussed my harping on the poor ethics of the governor and informed me that DiPrete was thin-skinned and vindictive. "Be careful," he warned. "They'll plant drugs on you if you continue your criticism of DiPrete."

It was a shocking threat, but I wasn't worried. I barely drank and was in bed early most nights. No one would believe that I used drugs. Still, I was relieved when the governor was defeated on a 70-30 percent vote.

Several years later, the state was rocked by another major scandal. The colorful mayor of Providence, Vincent "Buddy" Cianci, was indicted on conspiracy to commit corruption charges. This man had been elected as a reformer in 1974 but was forced to resign his office in 1984 after pleading nolo contendere to an assault and battery charge. After Cianci divorced his wife and signed a financial settlement, he learned she had been having an affair with a local man. Furious that he had been duped into giving her money over his own affairs, Cianci summoned that man to his aptly named Power Street house. In the presence of a police officer, the outraged mayor spat on the guy, threatened him with a burning fireplace ember, and hit him. Questioned later after the encounter became public, Cianci did not deny the assault had taken place but claimed he was defending the honor of his family. As part of the plea agreement, Cianci resigned his mayorship and shortly thereafter became the area's most popular talk radio show host.

For six years, he kept his name in the public spotlight and slowly rehabilitated his image. In 1990 the incumbent mayor ran for governor, which created an opportunity for Cianci to resume his old job. In what has to rank as the political comeback of the decade in the Ocean State, Cianci won a tightly contested three-way race and reclaimed the mayor's office.

For a decade, Cianci presided over the renaissance of Providence. The city that had long been the ugly duckling of New England cities now became a destination city, with great restaurants and theaters and a downtown with a new mall and a relocated river.

But several years into office, he was indicted. According to federal investigators, Cianci's chief of staff and closest political confidant was seen on a videotaped recording accepting a cash bribe, and the mayor had been charged along with that man. The indictment alleged that Cianci had orchestrated a criminal conspiracy. City Hall was being run as a criminal enterprise for the enrichment of Cianci and his top aides.[3]

For months, the case dominated the headlines. Would the mayor be found guilty and sent to prison? The case put me on the NBC *Today Show* where, asked to assess the mayor's character, I said there was "a good Buddy and a bad Buddy." The good side of this man had presided over one of the most impressive urban rejuvenations in the Northeast. Rivers had been moved, a new mall had been built, and the city looked great.

However, at the same time, bad Buddy Cianci was mean and vindictive and often tried to screw his enemies. Cross him, and you would pay a serious price. He controlled everything that happened in the city, and the joke was that not a leaf fell in Providence without the mayor knowing about it.[4] Eventually, Cianci was convicted on federal corruption charges and sent to jail for several years.

What happened in Rhode Island occurred on a much grander scale nationally. Over several decades, the country has seen the rise of big money in politics, secret campaign contributions, and a Supreme Court decision known as *Citizens United* that opened gaping loopholes allowing the wealthy to influence elections. It was a corrupt system that harmed ordinary Americans and made them completely cynical.

A wealthy friend of mine described how to gain political influence through what he called a "get a Senator" strategy. Because of Senate rules granting unbridled authority to individual senators to block nominations through secret holds, object to "unanimous consent" motions, and engage in filibusters (that is, block action through unlimited debate), a popular tactic among those with extensive wealth was to develop a close relationship with a senator from a key committee and persuade that person to block undesired nominations or bills.[5]

Holds can be used to stop legislation that a senator doesn't like. Republican Senator Rand Paul of Kentucky, for example, was unhappy with a proposed treaty that would force Swiss banks to release the names of 22,000 wealthy Americans who have hidden an estimated $10 billion in offshore accounts. Even though the treaty was likely to win the approval of the Senate as a whole, for several years Paul single-handedly prevented action because he believed the new rules would invade personal privacy.[6]

With the "get a senator" strategy, a business leader needs only to obtain the support of a single member to prevent the chamber from taking a particular action. In a system of fragmented representation, having a senator who acts on one's behalf is an effective way to stymie unwanted government action or delay appointments affecting particular industries. Along with lobbyists who represent businesses and other vested interests, those who are rich and connected can stop measures deemed detrimental to their pocketbooks.

Billionaires enlist senators to write letters to federal regulators asking for investigations of competitors. An example of this came to light in the case of hedge fund manager William Ackman, of Pershing Square Capital Management. For years, the billionaire financier has run a campaign against the nutritional supplement firm Herbalife, alleging that its sales practices amount to an illegal pyramid scheme. Ackman has invested $1 billion in his belief that the company is overvalued.[7]

Not content with drawing his own conclusions regarding the business practices of Herbalife, he persuaded Democratic Senator Edward Markey of Massachusetts to write letters to the Securities and Exchange Commission and the Federal Trade Commission criticizing the firm and demanding a formal investigation. Ackman personally lobbied Markey's staff and hired a Markey aide to join his lobbying team. As soon as Markey's letter was made public, the Herbalife stock price dropped by 14 percent, partly achieving the billionaire's goals.

Through this and other means, the average person can see how political insiders win favorable treatment, bills include amendments that enrich certain corporations, and the rich have extraordinary access to the top levels of government. It is a virulent feature of the entire system.

Upset with special influence, candidate Trump promised to drain "the swamp," as he loved to refer to Washington, D.C. Trump campaigned as a reformer who would shake things up and end public corruption. Speaking around the country, he claimed the system was rigged against ordinary people and past leaders were corrupt to the core.

Yet after winning the presidency, Trump demonstrated blatant disregard for ethical standards. He dined regularly at his own Trump Hotel in Washington, D.C., and foreign embassies and conservative groups hosted their events at this property, thereby funneling money to the president. Ditto for his golf courses and restaurants. Scarcely a week went by without Trump promoting his personal businesses or drawing attention to one of his properties.

His supporters looked the other way, but his opponents were out-raged. They could not understand why moralistic organizations that emphasized strong ethics and family values overlooked Trump's ethi-cal lapses and personal misconduct. Many of these very same organi-zations had condemned Clinton and Obama for ethical improprieties yet were strangely silent in the face of grand indiscretions on Trump's part. In a polarized atmosphere, it was hard for Trump haters to un-derstand why other voters did not share their outrage.

College Admissions

It is not just politics that has been afflicted by insider dealings. Novel forms of favoritism have arisen in regard to college admissions, es-pecially at elite private institutions. I started teaching at Brown University in 1982, and a decade earlier, the school had undergone a student-led revolution. Dissatisfaction with the status quo drove many pupils to complain about the highly structured, old-style cur-riculum. Fueled by the energy of the anti–Vietnam War, civil rights, feminist, and environmental movements, a wave of change washed over Brown and other universities around the country.

Rather than fight the shift, the faculty, trustees, and administra-tors adopted a series of reforms developed by students Ira Magaziner and Elliot Maxwell known as the New Curriculum. This revamping did away with all core courses and distribution requirements that forced students to take courses in a variety of areas. The alteration meant undergraduates would not have to take courses they dreaded, such as math, foreign languages, or natural science.

In addition, the university abolished the grades of D and F, along with pluses and minuses. There would be no failure at Brown, just not getting credit for a course. Thereafter, students would be graded on a scale of A, B, C, or No Credit. The rationale was that to encour-age experimentation outside one's specialty, students should be free to take courses without a fear of flunking and to avoid the risk of a bad mark on their transcript.

The impact of these changes on the university was profound. When it had a structured curriculum and distribution requirements, Brown was in the middle of the pack on college ratings. If you got the same type of education at Brown as you might get at Harvard, Stanford, or the University of Chicago, there was no reason to prefer Brown over bigger schools with a stronger reputation.

But when the school changed to an unstructured curriculum, no distribution requirements, and a simplified grading system, Brown became the best of that genre. It was a marketer's dream. You want more student choice, more curricular options, and flexible requirements? Then come to Brown.

This brilliant bit of countercyclical programming catapulted Brown into national and international prominence and turned the university into one of the most popular schools in the country. Students loved the curricular choices and the flexibility. Rather than being told what to study, they could choose the courses in which they were most interested.

By 1983, the *New York Times* proclaimed the university the "hottest" school in the land. In a March 20 story titled "Brown Outpacing Rivals in Ivy League Popularity," reporter Fox Butterfield noted that Brown was receiving more applications than Harvard, Yale, or Princeton.

One applicant explained her preference for Brown over Princeton. "I didn't want to be told what I had to take," she noted. Dean of admissions Eric Widmer also pointed to the open curriculum. "There ought to be an alternative to the Harvard plan, proscribing what amounts to distribution in an age when knowledge has proliferated to such an extent there can't be agreement about it," he pointed out.[8]

Applications soared, and it became very difficult to gain admission. Its unstructured curriculum and desirable East Coast location were attractive to potential students, and thousands of applicants competed for the 1,500 slots open each year.

Within a decade, Brown would have an acceptance rate in the single digits and become the school of the rich and famous. Having a low admissions rate demonstrated that Brown was a highly desirable place to attend. Those who were admitted felt like they were quite special.

The New Curriculum not only drew large numbers of applicants to the university, it also transformed the type of student who enrolled. Rather than attracting the children of the affluent who wanted to maintain the status quo, Brown became the choice of young people who wanted to change society and politics. The unstructured curriculum attracted smart, creative, and independent-minded students who were talented and entrepreneurial.

Some of the admitted students (and their parents) were celebrities in their own right. At my first Brown commencement, I was thrilled to see Jackie Kennedy. Dressed all in black for the Campus Dance, she exuded grace and privilege as she sat by the dance floor. Few people went up to talk to her, but we all gawked at the Camelot icon.

Of course, everyone on campus was distraught years later when young John Kennedy's private plane crashed, and the heir to the legend was lost forever. Speaking to me after the plane crash, one of his advisers mused about the possible source of Kennedy's disorientation as pilot.

Unbeknownst to most people, John was dyslexic. Doing numbers and distinguishing between left and right were problems for him. This malady was one of the reasons he had done poorly in school and twice flunked his bar exam. He was not stupid, he just had an untreated learning disability.[9] His dyslexia had only recently been diagnosed, and this adviser and I both wondered whether on that fateful flight to Martha's Vineyard, John's spatial disorientation had caused his fatal navigational errors.

Amy Carter didn't fare so well at Brown, although for a very different reason. She devoted most of her time to political protesting and didn't go to class. She eventually left school without a degree. For a little while, though, she stayed around Providence. Annie was once buying a piece of jewelry at a local shop when she noticed the sales clerk was Amy. If not for her recognizable face, one would have mistaken her for any other young shop attendant with uncombed hair and scraggly looks.

Sometimes, celebrity students produced interesting quandaries for the faculty. In 1988, just as her father was seeking the presidential nomination, Kara Dukakis took my campaigns and elections class. After the first class, she came up and introduced herself. I welcomed her to the course and asked if it were okay if occasionally I told jokes making fun of her father. Smiling, she replied, "Sure. In fact, there are some jokes I could tell you about him."

People want to think admissions decisions at elite institutions always are made on the basis of merit. And most of the time, at Brown, that was the case. Ivy League schools had rigorous admissions standards and employed dozens of people to read each file and assess applicant's suitability for the university. Most of each year's class was filled with highly deserving students.

Yet there were exceptions to this fact. The children of the rich and famous received special treatment, as did the children of alumni. If your parent or grandparent had gone to the university, your chances of gaining admission were greatly enhanced. The thought was a family's loyalty to the institution should be rewarded, even though that created unfairness with other applicants. Ultimately, there would be a book by Daniel Golden entitled *The Price of Admission* that explained how Brown and other Ivies had risen to prominence in part based on "affirmative action" directed at wealthy donors and famous celebrities.[10]

Years later, a lawsuit at Harvard University accusing the school of unfair admissions would confirm a number of questionable practices. Documents unsealed by that lawsuit showed how Harvard privileged the applications of the wealthy, donors, legacies (that is, alumni offspring), and faculty children. As an example, the admission rate for legacies was 33.6 percent, compared to 5.9 percent of non-alumni applicants.[11]

In addition, the university had a "dean's list" or "director's list" that allowed top school administrations to tip the balance of mar-

ginal applicants toward admission. The tilt could be based on expectations of a donation, having a famous relative, or having met the
applicant at a recruitment event.[12] Under oath, the dean of admissions was forced to explain e-mails he had sent "suggesting special
consideration for the offspring of big donors, those who have 'already
committed to a building' or have 'an art collection which could con-
ceivably come our way.'"[13]

At Brown, I saw similar practices firsthand. When these students
came to campus for admissions tours, the development office would
call me and other faculty members to set up special meetings. On
many occasions, I met the children of famous politicians and media
celebrities who wanted their son or daughter to get into Brown. I
talked with them about the university, and sometimes wrote letters
on their behalf.

The parents of these individuals populated our lecture series and
campus events. Democratic presidential candidate and Brown parent
John Kerry spoke at the university. Reporters complained about how
aloof and standoffish he was during his campaign. Yet at our event,
the defeated candidate was warm, gracious, and generous with his
time. For an hour after his speech, he signed autographs and posed
for pictures.

One of the most surprising celebrities I met was the famed actor
and Brown parent Dustin Hoffman. When he appeared at a Parent's
Weekend speech, I was shocked to discover how short the man was.
Although officially listed as five feet, six inches tall, he appeared even
shorter than that. No one was talking to him after the lecture so I
went up and introduced myself as a faculty member in political science. Hoffman immediately struck me as a shy person. I asked him
whether his son was having a good experience at Brown. "Yes, he
loves Brown," the actor replied. "He is having a great time and things
are working out really well for him."

We had just heard an American politics lecture by television
broadcaster Chris Matthews, and Hoffman was scheduled to address
parents the following night about his theater experiences. I asked

him if he was excited to be speaking at Brown. "No," was his answer. "I am very nervous." Hoffman explained that it was difficult for him to give public speeches and he admired Matthews's ability to go up on stage and be funny and opinionated in his comments.[14]

Of course, this turned out to be false modesty on the actor's part. The next night, he wowed the crowd with tales of Hollywood and his own background. He started his speech by insisting he was not a lecturer. A teacher is someone who knows, he said. "I never did and still don't know." He explained how he went into acting after a friend at his community college told him, "Nobody flunks acting. It's like gym."[15]

The two-time Academy Award winner pointed out to the audience how his acting experiences had informed his life. Speaking of his part in the movie *Tootsie,* where he dressed up as a woman, he noted how a group of men had come up to him on the set, looked him up and down, and immediately "erased" him in favor of younger, more attractive women. Even though he confessed that he had done the same thing in his personal life, the experience showed how hurtful this was. Even when he as a man was dressed up like a woman, he noted, "You want to feel attractive. You want to feel sexy." It was years later that Hoffman was accused of taking advantage of women who wanted an acting career.

On another occasion, I was surprised at a commencement party to meet the five-time Emmy winner and Brown parent Candice Bergen. The star of the hit situation comedy *Murphy Brown,* Bergen was down-to-earth and inquisitive. Rather than being a prima donna, which would have been understandable given her extraordinary achievements, she peppered me with questions about Brown. What is it like teaching there? How did I find the students? After some of the figures I had met, it was refreshing to meet a famous entertainer with no arrogance.

I told Bergen how creative and talented our students were. She already knew this because of a daughter at the university. She noted that she had once attended her daughter's comparative literature seminar. However, the class did not hold her attention, and she was embarrassed to fall asleep in front of the students.

At the university, I met the first of several billionaires in the form of legendary broadcaster Ted Turner. He had attended the university three decades earlier, and although he had been kicked out in the 1960s for disciplinary code violations involving alcohol and women, years later Brown had awarded him an honorary degree in recognition of his development of CNN, the first all-news cable network. Pleased with the honor, Turner had funded a faculty position and pledged a multimillion-dollar gift to the school. That made him what Brown euphemistically called a "friend" of the university.

Accompanied by his then-wife, Jane Fonda, he came to campus in 1995 to give a lecture about the environment entitled "Our Common Future." Turner was alternately serious, funny, and outrageous. He explained the importance of the environment to the future of humanity and talked about why he was raising buffalo on his huge Montana ranch. Then, in an unexpected twist, he joked that what he really liked about living in the West was being able to "take a whiz" off his front porch. The Ivy League audience laughed uproariously at the crude joke.

Turning back to his broader message, he related the lessons of his life. His most difficult challenge, he said, had been making the first million dollars; after that, everything was easy. Money begets money, he bluntly observed, thereby making it possible to gain even greater wealth through social and political connections. Wealth enables rich people to convert financial might into political power or social influence. It was an honest but insightful comment regarding financial influence in contemporary life.

Around the same time, we had Democratic political consultant James Carville speak on campus. He opened with a series of jokes. On his stint in the Marine Corps, the Cajun said he had achieved the rank of corporal. This made him, he said, "the highest-ranking military person in the Clinton administration." And on his dating and eventual marriage to GOP consultant Mary Matalin, he noted that his colleagues kidded him that "the only thing James Carville likes to do with Republicans is beat them and date them." When the crowd tittered at the vague reference to domestic violence, Carville had a quick retort. "Oh no, the P.C. crowd will be after me for that one."

More surprising was Paul Wellstone, the liberal Democrat with a reputation for speaking up for the downtrodden. Wellstone was one of my heroes. I had an autographed picture of him in my office. He was highly principled, spoke up against injustice when others trembled, and presented himself as a spokesperson for the little guy. He was exactly the type of public official I admired.

Yet in person, I saw another side to Wellstone. He had agreed to go to dinner following the talk with a small number of students. Driving him over to Federal Hill to go to an Italian restaurant, his student driver got lost. Wellstone became very irate and told the student the evening was over and he no longer would go to dinner with him. "Take me back to the hotel," he demanded, and he would eat there alone with his wife. The stunned students took him back to the hotel. As he reached the hotel, he turned to the students and said he needed $60 for dinner. The disappointed students gave him the cash and left him at the hotel. For a man who claimed to speak for the little guy, this was a shabby way to deal with inexperienced young people.

Earlier in the day, I had a similar experience with him. Before his arrival, I had tried to book him in the city's luxury hotel. But his Washington staff had vetoed that plan and said, "Paul wants to stay on campus." Brown had a beautiful old building with antiques-filled rooms and four-poster beds reserved for dignitaries, so I booked him there. When we arrived at the lodging, though, Wellstone took one look at the old-fashioned bed and declared, "I can't sleep on that. Take me to a nice hotel." Not wanting to disappoint the senator, I did as he instructed.

Philanthropy

Fundraising is an area where money and connections clearly open doors. One of the wealthy people I met at Brown was A. Alfred Taubman. Estimated by Forbes to be a billionaire several times over, he was the donor whose $2 million gift had established the Taubman Center for American Policy and Political Institutions at Brown University in 1984. Ten years later, Taubman had come to a campus party honoring the anniversary of the center. There were panels showcasing center faculty and students and a social gathering for people in the community.

Governor Bruce Sundlun, then in the depths of his unpopularity owing to the state's banking crisis and about to be defeated for his party's renomination, came to the party. The first thing he did was seek out Taubman, who was standing by my side. Sundlun was a blunt and direct man who always came immediately to the point. He never bothered with small talk or social niceties. He was upset because I had just commented on the radio that his popularity was so low that Mickey Mouse could beat him.

Seeing me, it was clear the governor was not amused at my feeble joke. He turned to Taubman and said, "You no longer should fund the Taubman Center." Glaring, Sundlun pointed to me and told Taubman, "This guy doesn't know what he is doing." This is not exactly what you want the governor of your home state to be telling your leading donor. I was embarrassed and Taubman said little in response to this critique.

Shortly thereafter, Taubman did cut off his funding to the Taubman Center, but it had nothing to do with Sundlun's attack. Unbeknownst to any of us at the time, the shopping mall magnate was experiencing a major liquidity crisis. Real estate values had crashed around the country in the early 1990s, and Taubman was locked in a tight squeeze. He owned Sotheby's auction house and two dozen upscale shopping malls. The recession had weakened Taubman's financial position. He later would be convicted of price collusion and spend a year in federal prison.

As the new director of the Taubman Center, I received several calls from reporters asking if we were going to remove Taubman's name from our program. The answer was no, we weren't going to take his name off our center. We weren't going to do that, nor were Harvard or the University of Michigan, where Taubman also had made generous contributions.

Over the course of the preceding years, universities recruited many business leaders for their governing boards as part of a grand strategy to raise money. These individuals contributed large sums of money to sponsor particular activities. It was the corporatization of higher education. Although many outsiders see colleges as education institutions, increasingly they are being run like businesses. The new finance and business people who sat on college boards wanted universities to become more entrepreneurial and focused on external fundraising.

For many, this was a negative trend that implied universities no longer were focused on learning for its own sake but instead placed the emphasis on raising money. There would be a dominance of money over ideas, and a growth in financial conflicts of interest. Critics decried the inversion of priorities and longed for the good old days when professors could teach classes without worrying about financial imperatives.

For me personally, though, I became the beneficiary of this new emphasis on fundraising. In 1992 I was sitting at home at 7:30 a.m. when the phone rang. It was a local businessman whom I did not know who said his name was John Hazen White Sr. He owned a local factory that made water circulators and heating pumps and was concerned about corruption in Rhode Island politics. He invited me to visit his factory.

Normally, I don't meet strangers who call my house requesting a meeting. Over the years, I had been called by a number of wackos who had seen me on television and wanted to express their own opinions. One memorable guy informed me early one morning that I was "an asshole who doesn't know anything about politics."

But something in this businessman's voice made me take his request seriously. There was a sincerity that suggested this was not your typical nuisance call. I agreed to meet with him at his factory shortly afterward to find out what he wanted. We started talking and discovered we liked each other a lot.

Both of us deplored the poor ethics of Rhode Island politics. There was too much corruption and a lack of understanding of major policy issues. The Ocean State had too many examples of politicians enriching themselves at the expense of the general public. Something major needed to be done.

He expressed an interest in supporting our public policy center and wanted to know how he could help. John was the first rich guy who had posed that particular question to me. I did not know what to do so I called the Brown development office. They looked up his past giving patterns and discovered the previous year he had contributed $25 to the university's John Carter Brown Library. Not knowing what he was interested in, they suggested he support the Library or student financial aid. I called John back and relayed that information.

That night, I thought about the day's events and realized I was being completely stupid. Some guy wanted to give money to our program and I was turning him over to the library? That made no sense.

I called Tom Anton, then the director of the Taubman Center, and we hatched a new plan. John had called me because he had seen a state public opinion poll on public attitudes toward government officials, demonstrating how unhappy citizens were with state government. He liked the idea of polling because it was a way to provide a mechanism of accountability for government officials.

Anton and I decided we would give John three options. In the development world, it is always good to provide a menu of choices so funders have a range of options. The first option was a gift of $100,000 that would underwrite a series of surveys over several years. The second option was a donation of $250,000 that would cover more surveys over a longer period of time. The third option would be a gift of $500,000, which would go into the university endowment and allow us to spend 5 percent of the principal in perpetuity on the polling operation. If he liked the third possibility, we would rename our polling operation the John Hazen White Public Opinion Laboratory and refer to it that way in our press releases and public events.

I faxed John a two-page proposal laying out the three options. The next day I was surprised to get a call from the businessman. I worried he would feel insulted by the outrageous amounts of money we were asking, but to my surprise, he opened the conversation by thanking me for the proposal. In a quiet voice, he then said, "I'd like to go for the third option." I couldn't believe my good fortune. He was going to provide a $500,000 endowment gift for our public opinion laboratory.

Anton and I were ecstatic, but there was one little detail about which to worry. The development office had not been consulted and it still thought John was going to give money for the John Carter Brown Library. We quickly informed Director Sam Babbitt of what we had done. He was highly upset and said the faculty was not allowed to solicit money that way. He would have to talk to President Vartan Gregorian.

For a few days, we held our breath. Would the money be taken away or redirected to another program? Finally, it was decided Brown would accept John's $500,000 gift for the polling operation. Part of the reasoning was that since John previously had made only token contributions of $25 to the university, this almost certainly would be his only gift. Since we already had solicited his agreement, it made sense for the university to accept the arrangement.

It surprised everyone when over the course of the next few years, John and his son John Jr. contributed a total of $6 million to the university's Taubman Center. In a series of gifts, the family agreed to support a lecture series that would bring prominent speakers to campus, a public policy internship program, two endowed professorships, a postdoctoral fellow program, and a master's program in public policy. In a short period of time, he had gone from a $25 contribution to providing us with millions of dollars.

For the internship money, we had to out-negotiate the university's provost, Frank Rothman. He felt the gift should go toward students across the university, not just public policy undergraduates. He realized John was a much more generous donor than anyone anticipated, and it was time to move him from the domain of the Taubman Center to the university as a whole. This was an immediate crisis for me because it meant our program would get no more of his money.

At that time, neither Gregorian nor Rothman had a close personal relationship with John, but I did. John and I had become close friends over a period of several years, and we talked once a week. We trusted each other with gossip about area politicians and generally found we thought the same way about the corruption of state politics.

I called John to discuss his approach to philanthropy. "There are two ways to undertake gift giving," I told him. "You could spread your money out among several beneficiaries or you could target your contributions on a single place and really have an impact." Since he had been building support for our programs at the Taubman Center, I argued the latter was a way to get more bang for his buck. Like most donors, John wanted to know that his money was being used effectively and making a difference in the community.

John was scheduled to meet with President Gregorian later that day. I knew something about Gregorian that worked to my advantage. Although he had a reputation as an outstanding fundraiser, he actually didn't like asking people for money. In his own words, he was a "trapper, not a skinner." By that, he meant that he was good at cultivating people and bringing them to support the university, but he didn't like the actual conversation where you asked a donor for a specific gift.

Armed with this knowledge, I told John when he met with the president, Gregorian would ask him what he wanted done with his gift. I advised him to tell the president he wanted to continue supporting public policy so he could target his gifts and really have an impact on the community. My plan worked to perfection. Even though Gregorian agreed with Rothman that the money should go to the university, not the Taubman Center, he did not press John to redirect his gift. When John announced he preferred to give the money for public policy internships, that became the ultimate decision because Gregorian respected the donor's preferences.

At Brookings, I had many encounters with wealthy individuals owing to our location in the nation's capital. Donors understood that our work had discernible impact and wanted to support the high-quality work of our scholars. We won grants from leading foundations as well as prominent companies and individuals. Over time, between Brown and Brookings, I would raise more than $41 million.

With the support of John Hazen White Jr., we launched a global manufacturing initiative. It analyzed how the United States compared with other countries in its policies, regulations, and infrastructure investment. Once a year, we held a forum and invited experts from various aspects of the manufacturing field.

The Bill & Melinda Gates Foundation provided funding for projects on financial inclusion and global health. After making his fortune at Microsoft, Bill Gates had launched this enterprise and it quickly became the largest foundation in the United States. His staff would embody the tenets of impact philanthropy and constantly ask us how we were having an impact. His program officers wanted research that would change the world and pressed hard on achieving actual change, not just talking about the problem.

Sometimes, Brookings's fundraising practices drew outside criticism. In 2016 Eric Lipton and Brooke Williams, of the *New York Times*, wrote a front-page article accusing Brookings of engaging in questionable practices. It noted that one of our programs had accepted a gift from a San Francisco real estate developer and named him a senior fellow. The reporters claimed that was unethical and a sign of undue corporate influence.[16]

Our administrative team scrambled after this disclosure to tighten our gift agreements and make sure that never happened again. We had meetings to discuss our fundraising practices, how to safeguard them, and make sure they were in accord with our claims of independent research. It was a useful warning that reporters were paying attention and we should maintain high fundraising standards.

A couple of years later, another funding controversy struck. *Washington Post* columnist Jamal Khashoggi was writing negative pieces about his native Saudi Arabia regarding its authoritarian rule and corrupt practices. But needing documents for his upcoming wedding, he had gone to the Saudi consulate in Istanbul, Turkey. Awaiting him was a fifteen-person Saudi hit team that tortured and killed him. For weeks, the Saudi government lied about Khashoggi's fate and falsely claimed he had left the consulate on his own and they didn't know what had happened to him. Eventually, though, when there was no sign of the journalist, the Saudis were forced to admit they had killed him.

The barbaric episode attracted worldwide attention and a searing indictment of the Saudi government and Crown Prince Mohammad Bin Salman. The authoritarian regime had a poor record on human rights, treated women poorly, and was engaged in a brutal war against Yemen. The Khashoggi murder led to widespread condemnation of Saudi Arabia and media scrutiny over Saudi finances. It didn't take long for enterprising reporters to notice that along with many universities, lobbyists, and influence operations, Brookings had received Saudi money for a research study of think tanks. Brookings president John Allen quickly announced that the institution was returning the money and would not accept any further gifts from the Saudi kingdom.[17] It was important to take a strong ethical stance on this issue.

EIGHT

OVERCOMING HYPERCONFLICT

Many political, economic, and cultural factors have intensified hyperconflict over the years and made it difficult for opposing forces to understand one another. This includes major political gyrations, disruptive economic shifts, the loss of educational opportunities, identity politics, religious tensions, a backlash against globalization and immigration, and concerns regarding special influence by the wealthy.

According to Julia Azari, the United States has moved into a situation where "the issues we fight over—gender, race, immigration, culture and the role of government—divide Americans neatly and consistently under party labels. The current moment feels divisive because major policy and political questions are 'sorted' between the parties—Republicans are mostly unified around one set of answers, and Democrats are mostly unified around another."[1]

As a result of these disagreements, our system faces a number of risks. They include widespread polarization, diverging identities, mistrust and intolerance, a tendency to define opponents as enemies, political sorting on the part of many Americans, and a decline of facts in civil discourse. Unless we can bridge hyperconflict and forge a new path, it will be hard to maintain democracy and make progress on national and international challenges.

Widespread Polarization

The rise of political polarization has produced a Congress with virtually no centrists. Figure 8-1 shows the percentage of House members who are considered politically moderate in their voting patterns, and the drop over recent decades has been precipitous.[2] In the 1950s, around 60 percent of Republicans and Democrats had centrist orientations. But by the late 1980s and early 1990s, only about one-third

FIGURE 8-1

Share of Moderates in U.S. House of Representatives, by Party, 1950–2014

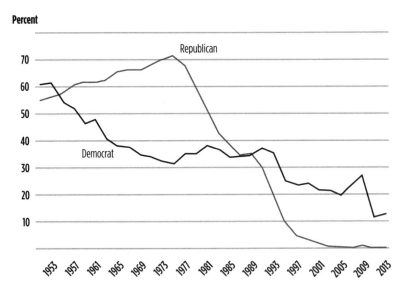

Source: Keith Poole, "The Polarization of the Congressional Parties," Legacy Vote View, March 21, 2015 (https://legacy.voteview.com/political_polarization_2014 .htm).

were moderate. In recent years, moderates have gone virtually extinct, as currently there are none in the GOP House delegation and only 10 percent in the Democratic caucus.

The near extinction of moderates has had detrimental consequences for U.S. governance. Bargaining, compromise, and negotiation used to be the guiding principles for American politicians. Legislators sought to resolve conflict, handle differences of opinion, and forge winning coalitions that cut across a variety of perspectives.

Sadly, that is no longer the case. Politicians fight with everything they have, and conflict resolution has become a matter of might more than of right. Adversaries seek to win at all costs and impose their views on the system. Compromise is seen as a betrayal of basic principles, not a reasonable way to reconcile differing opinions.

A Pew Research Center survey demonstrated the negative views of the opposition that have emerged. When asked why they identified with their party, 71 percent of Republicans and 63 percent of Democrats said the reason was the other party's policies were harmful for the country. In addition, more than one-third (37 percent among Republicans and 36 percent for Democrats) indicated they did not have much in common with people from the other party.[3]

In another poll, political scientist Jaime Settle found that political orientation was even affecting social relationships. She asked a public opinion sample if they would be upset if their child married someone from another party; 50 percent of Republicans and 33 percent of Democrats answered in the affirmative.[4]

Diverging Identities

For the nation as a whole, sharp differences have emerged in people's basic identities. For example, people who live in small-town America love traditional values and the helpfulness that neighbors provide for one another. In a Facebook post, Carolyn described her rural community in the following terms:

College Corner could be considered a one-horse town. But the horse we rode in on has wings. A couple of weeks ago Deana had a tree fall on the road and friends and neighbors came in and helped late in the evening. David posted asking for help with his practicals for his EMT class and got lots of volunteers. When we had the Town cleanup you saw older folks helping younger folks and younger folks helping older folks. The town was full of volunteers helping each other. Recently a friend fell in her front yard and couldn't get up. Someone stopped and helped her get up. Local churches go together every year to supply milk for kids who otherwise wouldn't get any. Last year they supplied over 6,500 milks for kids in College Corner, Liberty, and Oxford. And the list goes on. We may not be perfect but living here gives almost a daily example of all that is good about the human race.[5]

Echoing that sentiment, one of our childhood friends commented that "small towns have large hearts. . . . We were there for each other."[6]

That sense of community has not always been the case in the places where I lived as an adult. City life has many advantages amid the plethora of movies, restaurants, theater, sports, and music, but many urbanites feel unrooted, with a lack of the kind of community I experienced growing up on the farm. People go their own separate ways, and there are few connections that bind people together.

A 2017 survey undertaken by professors Shibley Telhami and Stella Rouse of the University of Maryland shows the vast gulf in people's partisan orientation. When asked which identities were most important to them, Republicans cited their religious views while Democrats pointed to a cosmopolitan viewpoint focused on the world as a whole. Thirty-three percent of Republicans named their religious identity as most crucial, compared with 12 percent of Democrats. Only 7 percent of Republicans saw themselves as "citizens of the world" compared with 34 percent of Democrats who felt that way. When asked if they viewed their identity as being a citizen of the United States, 53 percent of Republicans agreed, while only 35 percent of Democrats responded that way.[7]

Differences in personal identity affect how people feel about a variety of issues. Those who identified closely with being an American are much more likely to express positive views about Confederate monuments and approve of President Trump's comments about the two-sidedness of violence during the Charlottesville protests. The same is true regarding income inequality as those who see themselves being American are less likely to complain about the wealth gap and less apt to think there has been a decline in U.S. upward mobility.[8]

Furthermore, national identifiers are more likely to accede to the current practice of opposing National Football League players who refuse to stand for the national anthem. The issue deeply divides the country by race, as 83 percent of professional football fans are white, while 70 percent of the players are African American.[9] In a Quinnipiac University survey, "63 percent of white Americans disapproved of anthem demonstrations, while 74 percent of black Americans approved."[10] These numbers help us understand the racial dimension of the player protests.

Public differences have even affected long-term evaluations of higher education. For example, a study found stark differences between Republicans and Democrats in their assessments of college professors. According to the Pew Research Center, when asked to rate them on a point scale of 0 to 100 (cold to warm), Republicans gave a score of 30, meaning a cool rating, compared with the much warmer score of 66 from Democrats.[11] In general, Democrats have more positive impressions of universities and feel that institutions of higher learning contribute to the United States, while Republicans worry about political correctness on campus and overly liberal professors.

Mistrust and Intolerance

Mistrust has not always been the prevailing sentiment in the United States. Figure 8-2 shows the trend regarding trust in the federal government.[12] When asked how much of the time you can trust government to do what is right, 73 percent in 1958 said most of the time or about always. But this number dropped to 36 percent in 1974, following the Watergate scandal with President Richard Nixon, and 21 percent in 1994, during the contentiousness of the Clinton administration. It rose to 56 percent in 2002, when the 9/11 terrorist attacks united the country. However, it fell back to 22 percent in 2012 in the aftermath of the Great Recession, when voters doubted leader veracity and wondered whose interests were being served.[13]

FIGURE 8-2

Trust in the Federal Government to Do What Is Right, 1958–2012

Source: University of Michigan, "Trust the Federal Government," *ANES Guide to Public Opinion and Electoral Behavior, 1958–2012.*

Poor economic performance and international setbacks have re-inforced public skepticism. Public disenchantment makes it difficult for people to trust the results of political deliberations. The common assumption is that leaders are corrupt and selfish and are not trying to help the general public. With stagnating incomes for many people, ordinary folks doubt their children will lead healthy and prosperous lives.

Each year, the Edelman Agency undertakes a survey asking people if they trust major institutions. Based on this research, its researchers find that

> trust in institutions in the United States [has] crashed [in 2018], posting the steepest, most dramatic general population decline the Trust Barometer has ever measured. It is no exag-geration to state that the U.S. has reached a point of crisis that should provoke every leader, in government, business, or civil sector, into urgent action. Inertia is not an option, and neither is silence. The public's confidence in the traditional structures of American leadership is now fully undermined and has been replaced with a strong sense of fear, uncertainty and disillusionment.[14]

This trend is problematic because of the partisan edge. A Pew Re-search Center study found that Republican voters were 19 percentage points more likely to trust the federal government during George W. Bush's administration but 16 percentage points less likely to trust it during Obama's administration.[15] This combination of partisanship and mistrust represents a toxic mix for American society.

Opponents as Enemies

Democracy does not perform well when opponents see one another as enemies. As politics becomes a blood sport, it changes the nature of the combat and the manner in which political and policy differences get resolved. Enemies do not negotiate; rather, they fight to an often bitter end, and the winner imposes its will on the loser.

In his recent book, Republican Senator Ben Sasse characterizes this as the "them" problem and asks the provocative question of "why we hate each other." He perceptively describes the "polarization business model" in which media outlets, advocacy groups, and political candidates make money and build support by identifying opponents as evildoers. Far too many leaders today have both economic and political reasons for fueling rage toward opponents.[16]

There are few shades of grey in a world culture so polarized. There is no room for people who see both sides of the disagreement. Each side has its own facts, and differences in impressions affect the way issues get addressed. This leads to what University of Maryland political scientist Lilliana Mason calls "partisan prejudice," or negative feelings about people from the opposite party.[17]

Harvard professors Steven Levitsky and Daniel Ziblatt worry a lot about this kind of orientation. They write,

> When societies divide into partisan camps with profoundly different worldviews, and when those differences are viewed as existential and irreconcilable, political rivalry can devolve into partisan hatred. Parties come to view each other not as legitimate rivals but as dangerous enemies. Losing ceases to be an accepted part of the political process and instead becomes a catastrophe. When that happens, politicians are tempted to abandon forbearance and win at any cost. If we believe our opponents are dangerous, should we not use any means necessary to stop them?[18]

In my youth, there was greater acceptance of opposing political viewpoints. For example, President John Kennedy was not popular in my hometown. As a northeastern Democrat, Kennedy was considerably to the left of prevailing sentiments in Fairhaven, Ohio. But when he was assassinated in 1963, nearly everyone, regardless of political perspective, mourned the loss. Fairhaven school students were let out of school early. According to my childhood friend Richard, "as [students] were walking down the hill from the Fairhaven school, someone commented they were glad the president was shot since it let them get out of school. It made [our friend] Dale mad and he threw the guy down the hill!"[19]

Today, political passions run strong, and it is not easy to defend opposing politicians. People circle the wagons around their own points of view and castigate anyone who is outside the circle. I have seen this on many occasions from both the Left and the Right. During a period of polarization, adversaries often find it difficult to say anything nice about one another.

Writing to me right after Trump won the presidency, my friend Linda graphically illustrated this tendency. She said, "I would want to leave the country if that lying bitch Hillary or socialist Bernie Sanders had won. And I wish those damn liberal movie stars would leave or else shut the fuck up and stick to acting. I just wish the liberal news would shut the fuck up and quit promoting bullshit."[20]

In 2018 evangelist Franklin Graham spoke at a religious gathering in California. In discussing the Democratic domination of the state, he said, "The blue wall of California represents secular values that have taken root on the country's west coast. Progressive? That's just another word for godless."[21] A Texas billboard echoed a similar sentiment when it proclaimed "Liberals. Please continue on I-40 until you have left our GREAT STATE OF TEXAS."[22]

The Trump presidency has taken social and cultural polarization to new heights. This conclusion was made clear to me when Joanne recommended a recent movie called *The Trump Prophecy*. It debuted in fall 2018 with the theme that Trump's election "was an act of God, who chose the philandering billionaire and reality TV star to restore America's moral values."[23] My sister saw the movie and raved about it. "[Trump] is called the chosen candidate because he was tapped by

God to bring God's precepts to life. . . . This is typical of how God does the unlikely thing," she preached.

In this situation, it is little surprise that public opinion data reveal that Democrats and Republicans have turned quite negative against one another. Emory University political scientist Alan Abramowitz analyzed changes over time and found that in 2012, party members rated their opponents a chilly 30 out of 100 on a feeling thermometer, compared with a much warmer 47 percent in 1978.[24] This shift toward "coolness" regarding the opposing party shows that parties no longer are a force of moderation in America but rather an accelerant of polarization and mistrust.

Although the United States has not broken down into warring camps or civil unrest, American society has moved toward a winner-take-all mentality that offers huge rewards for winners. That increases the stakes of policy and political battles and reinforces the view that the ends justify the means. Combatants no longer hold back in their choice of tactics because they fear their opponents will use everything that is available to them.

Yale University professor Amy Chua worries this kind of mentality will increase group conflict. She argues, "Today, no group feels completely dominant. Every group feels attacked, pitted against other groups not just for jobs and spoils but for the right to define the nation's identity. In these conditions, democracy devolves into zero-sum group competition." Hyperconflict brings out the worst in everyone, owing to the scope of disagreements and the high stakes of the battle. Winning becomes the total goal, to the exclusion of fair play or just outcomes.[25]

Mocking the caricatured nature of political divisions, humorist David Barry penned a satirical column that asked, "Do we truly believe that ALL red-state residents are ignorant racist fascist knuckle-dragging NASCAR-obsessed cousin-marrying, road-kill-eating tobacco-juice dribbling gun-fondling religious fanatic rednecks or that ALL blue-state residents are godless unpatriotic pierced-nose Volvo-driving France-loving left-wing Communist latte-sucking tofu-chomping holistic-wacko neurotic vegan weenie perverts?"[26] Today, the answer to his question seems to be in the affirmative. People in both parties have adopted strikingly unflattering views of one another.

Political Sorting

In a world defined by diverging identities, economic turmoil, and political divisions, people have sorted themselves into like-minded groups. Indeed, in a world of widespread "megachange," the safest strategy is to circle the wagons and join forces with people of similar backgrounds and perspectives.[27] The U.S. objective of a country based on tolerance and mutual understanding has given rise to gated communities, walled gardens, and political sorting. Many individuals prefer to associate with people who share their basic values, objectives, and interests and avoid people who do not share basic perspectives.

This tendency is true in both physical and digital worlds. In terms of the physical world, people often choose to live in areas that are racially, politically, or economically homogeneous. They prefer being surrounded by those with similar mentalities. Dealing with people from opposing points of view or backgrounds causes tensions that are hard to resolve.[28]

Sometimes, these boundaries revolve around racial lines. Research by the Public Religion Research Institute found that "if you looked at the average white person's 100 closest friends, you would find that 91 would be white. If you looked at the average black person's 100 closest friends, 83 of them would be black."[29]

With digital technology, it is very easy to isolate oneself. People can easily find politically reinforcing communities, whether liberal, conservative, fundamentalist, libertarian, green, or gay. Technology helps people overcome the limitations of geography and find the individuals who share their basic viewpoint and become even more tribal. An analysis of social-media tweeting by sociologists Eric Forbush and Nicol Turner Lee found a communications "echo chamber" in which people retweet within narrow political networks. They argue that this behavior promotes extremism and polarization.[30]

The problem, of course, with radical separation is the risk of mutual misunderstanding. It is hard to understand people from differing backgrounds when there is limited personal or social contact. Opinions are more likely to be stereotypical and based on what one thinks the other group is like rather than what they may actually be like. Caricatures create hidden or unconscious biases, and these stereotypes have consequences. With a low opinion of adversaries, it is easy to justify poor treatment of them.

The Decline of Facts

In 2015 a CNN/ORC survey found that 20 percent of U.S. adults and 43 percent of Republicans believed Barack Obama was a Muslim.[31] Even though the then-president publicly professed his Christian faith, a significant percentage did not believe him, choosing instead to accept a false impression. This poll shows how easy it is in the contemporary situation for people to develop their own facts, even when they are inaccurate.

Jennifer Kavanagh and Michael Rich of RAND Corporation describe this phenomenon as "truth decay," and they say it has intensified over the past two decades. They blame this development on the extremism of social media and diminished school time spent on media literacy and critical thinking.[32]

Democracy is at risk when facts are in dispute. My sister Shirley expressed this sentiment clearly when she told me, "Our country has gotten so bad that no one knows what is true. Everyone lies. The government is sleazy and dishonest."

Things have gotten so bad that Republicans and Democrats see very different economies. Surveys undertaken at the University of Michigan have found the perception gap on performance of the economy under Trump has widened between the parties to an extraordinary 56 percentage points, up from an average of 20 points during the Obama, Bush, and Reagan presidencies.[33] In 2018, with the national unemployment rate at 3.8 percent, Democrats think a recession is about to start, while Republicans believe the economy is strong and likely to continue growing.

Republican House Speaker Paul Ryan blames culture and technology for these fundamental differences in perspective. In a speech at the National Catholic Prayer Breakfast, he noted, "We see moral relativism becoming more and more pervasive in our culture. Identity politics and tribalism have grown on top of this. All of it has been made more prevalent by 21st century technology."[34]

I first noticed the move toward subjective versions of truth from humanities colleagues in the academy. A number of years ago, postmodern theories of society became quite common. The view was that truth was relative to your station in life and morality depended on your particular perspective. Unseen patriarchies and class structures blinded people to objective realities.[35]

The rise of social relativism moved academic and then civil discourse down a slippery path to post-truth politics and fake news. If there is no objectivity, there can be no universal truth. Life depends on interpretation and social constructions, and one person's construction is no better than another's. In a world unanchored by objective realities, it is hard to discern truth and separate fact from fiction.

Senator Daniel Patrick Moynihan was famous for noting that people are not entitled to their own facts, but in a divided society, that actually has become the norm.[36] With very different conceptions of what is happening and who is to blame for developments someone does not like, it becomes impossible for normal politics to operate. Leaders can no longer bargain, negotiate, or compromise their way out of policy disputes. Rather, grassroots forces compel them to go for the political jugular.

Reconciling Differences

To reduce conflict, there has to be basic trust, an agreement on facts, and the ability to work with people who have different points of view. Those are the essential ingredients of a democratic system, where everyone's view gets heard and people have to work out diverging points of view.

Societies that don't have these qualities often break down into violence or unrest. They are not able to reconcile differences and resolve conflict. It becomes simpler to fight things out and determine a winner. There is little equity, justice, or fairness in these situations, just a winner who allocates the spoils.

In extreme cases, countries that cannot tame hyperconflict break apart into violent unrest. Because they are not able to resolve tensions through conventional means, they resort to war or authoritarian remedies. They repress those with whom they disagree and get rid of political opponents.

Bringing people together is a high priority to avoid these kinds of dystopias. We have to find ways to reduce conflict and develop solutions that work across a variety of viewpoints. Accomplishing these tasks is necessary to avoid a calamitous future. It will take fundamental reforms to place the system on a less conflictual and more stable footing.

My immediate family is unusual in the breadth of its political and religious disagreements. The four siblings of my generation include an academic researcher who studies American politics, a gay brother who distrusts conservatives, and two sisters who are Christians supporting Donald Trump. We are about as far apart as a family could possibly be in twenty-first-century America.

Indeed, our current differences amaze me because we grew up in quite similar circumstances. We played together, went to church together, attended identical schools, and sometimes had the same teachers. Even today, we talk and e-mail regularly and keep in touch. I would never have predicted our lives would diverge as much as they have.

But as national conflict has intensified, our differences on politics, religion, and culture have widened. Social and political issues have driven my brother and me to the left, while my sisters remain solidly on the right. It is especially hard for my brother because he lives a lifestyle that until the past few years could have gotten him fired from the Florida elementary school where he taught until retirement.

Discussing this issue, Ken said, "We can't discuss politics. Joanne is fully aware of this." Yet at the same time, her political positions distressed him. "In her eyes, Trump can do no wrong. She overlooks his faults because she believes in what he is doing. Evangelicals have sold their soul on Trump," he complained.[37]

My views have shifted a lot during the course of my life. To Linda, I tried to explain how that had happened. I told her,

> My politics are more liberal than most of my family. That is mainly because I wouldn't have been able to afford college without loans from the federal government. I paid my own way through college and couldn't have done it without federal assistance. So that pushed me more in the direction of wanting the government to help those who need assistance to get an education and better their lives. I am exhibit A on the value of that kind of investment. I very easily could be working in an Eaton factory, making no money, and being very angry about life. I never would have ended up an alcoholic like Dale, but I can envision lots of other bad trajectories for my life.[38]

However, she did not buy this interpretation of my transition to more progressive views. In an e-mail, she said, "I hate to think the smartest guy from a Preble County farm really believes that [liberal] horse shit." Then, in a deft turn, she wondered if my political evolution came about because I'd been bought off by money. "I realize catering to the liberals has given you big financial gains," she noted. The best thing I could do to understand American politics, she advised, was to listen to Rush Limbaugh. "He is very good at articulating common sense. And quoting him in your book would be a big plus. I sure hope you listen to him every day or read his transcript, to help offset the liberal bullshit inside the beltway you have been exposed to, and contaminated with, since college."

To make sure I understood her perspective, she sent me an article from a conservative website, "Chicks on the Right," that explained the "liberal problem" in America. According to that site's analysis, progressives are responsible for many of our country's contemporary problems because they "hate the idea of personal responsibility, of capitalism, of earning your way. They shun Christianity, the sanctity of life, the first and second amendments, and the idea that a country isn't a country without borders."[39]

In light of America's current schism, one has to wonder whether political tensions will at some point make peaceful coexistence impossible. Will American communities experience the strife of the Civil War, when one relative would be fighting for the North and another for the South? Iowa Representative Steve King, a Republican, predicts that the country is headed toward a dramatic confrontation. In 2018 he tweeted, "America is heading in the direction of another Harpers Ferry [the abolitionist raid that sparked the Civil War]. After that comes Ft. Sumter."[40] America clearly is not at that point yet, but it is no longer inconceivable that conflict could escalate in some dramatic fashion and lead to earth-shattering differences.

Paul Gosar, a conservative Republican member of Congress from Arizona, faced the unusual situation this year of siblings who appeared in an ad urging voters not to support their brother's reelection. Siblings Tim, Jennifer, Gaston, Joan, Grace, and David were in a Democratic commercial criticizing their brother's right-wing views. "We gotta stand up for our good name," said brother David. "This is not who we are." Sister Grace noted, "I couldn't be quiet any longer, nor should any of us be. . . . It would be difficult to see my brother as anything but a racist." Joan chimed in with that "I think my brother has traded a lot of the values we had at our kitchen table." For his part, Representative Gosar responded with a sharp retort. "My siblings who chose to film ads against me are all liberal Democrats who hate President Trump. Stalin would be proud," he angrily complained.[41]

Similar familial divisions arose elsewhere. In Nevada, GOP gubernatorial candidate Adam Laxalt saw several cousins speak out against him. At a fundraising event, Monique Laxalt explained, "We feel an obligation to speak out in opposition to Adam Laxalt's candidacy" owing to his positions on gun control and taxes, among other issues. "We do not believe Adam Laxalt represents Nevadans or has the interests of our people at heart," she noted.[42]

In the aftermath of the Brett Kavanaugh Supreme Court hearings, Republicans spun the election narrative that an "angry mob" of liberal Democrats risked "out-of-control anarchy." They characterized the anti-Kavanaugh protests and shouting demonstrators as evidence of a country veering seriously off course and threatening American democracy.[43] However, a political science professor I know disputed this interpretation on Facebook, saying "Democrats are the 'mob'? Seriously? After Charlottesville? After the body-slamming of a reporter by a candidate? After rally upon rally at which people scream 'lock her up'? Sorry, but NO, NO, NO, and NO!!!!!"[44]

Republican strategist John Weaver jokingly explained what he thought was happening with his party's strategy. "It's aimed at firing up Fox viewers and the more strident elements of Trump's base; it's fearmongering. I'm sure there is some little old lady in Iowa who now keeps her doors locked because she thinks there's going to be some anarchist mob coming through Davenport," he argued.[45]

Republican senator Rand Paul fears a violent clash from all the antagonism. Speaking during a Kentucky radio interview, he warned, "I really worry that someone is going to be killed." Noting the dramatic increase in political passions and societal tensions, he predicted there "is going to be an assassination." He argued that "those ratcheting up the conversation . . . have to realize that they bear some responsibility if this elevates to violence."[46]

These fears intensified in October 2018 when explosive devices were mailed to Barack Obama, Joe Biden, Hillary Clinton, Eric Holder, Cory Booker, Kamala Harris, Maxine Waters, Robert DeNiro, and CNN, among others. Those who screened their mail discovered the pipe bombs attached to a timer, and they alerted law enforcement. A week earlier, a similar object was found in the mailbox of liberal philanthropist George Soros. President Trump quickly put out a statement denouncing the actions and saying "these terrorizing acts are despicable, and anyone responsible will be held accountable to the fullest extent of the law."[47] But CNN director Jeff Zucker criticized Trump for his divisive rhetoric, which Zucker felt contributed to the dangerous atmosphere. "There is a total and complete lack of understanding at the White House about the seriousness of their continued attacks on the media," he pointed out.[48] Within a few days, a Trump supporter was arrested for the threatening mailings.

That same week, two African Americans were shot in a Kentucky grocery store, and eleven Jews were gunned down in a Pittsburgh synagogue while the killer shouted he "wanted all Jews to die." The country seemed to be disintegrating into hatred and turmoil. Data compiled by the Anti-Defamation League found a "57 percent rise in anti-Semitic incidents in the United States in 2017."[49] The same thing was happening in Europe as well.

Throughout all this contentiousness, people used social media to express their own views about American politics. My friend Bob jokingly posted a Facebook update alerting people there had been a major change in the 2018 electoral calendar. Republicans were to vote on Tuesday, November 6, he said, while Democrats should cast their ballots on Thursday, November 8. Linda meanwhile exhorted her Facebook friends to "vote Republican. They may not be perfect, but the other team's insane." Not to be outdone, my liberal friend Janette told her Facebook followers, "In keeping with the new spirit of America, I removed all the Jews, Arabs, Africans and immigrants from my Nativity scene. Nothing but sheep left, led by a jackass. Sounds about right."

Those communiqués were a sign of how sentiments were changing. Conflict was becoming more intense on all sides. I was not surprised because irreconcilable conflict had happened once before in my family at a time of extreme national turmoil. Nearly a century ago, my mother's family ruptured over economic tensions generated by the Great Depression. Following the death of my great-grandfather Robert Steele in 1926, my great-grandmother Emma Steele struggled to earn a living taking care of other people while her son, my grandfather Harry Steele, eked out a meager existence on the family farm.

Eventually, he was forced during the Depression to take out a bank loan and asked his sisters Mae, Georgia, and Martha to cosign the note since all of them were going to inherit the farm. That request led to harsh words and accusations that my grandfather was running the farm into the ground. Georgia's husband, John Thompson, told Emma that her family "had never been taught thrift and that was the reason some of you don't have anything."[50] Hearing those insults and other threatening words, my grandfather later said if John made those claims again, he would have him arrested.

Extraordinary national events produce great personal strain that divides families and nations. When there are difficult political or economic circumstances, it is hard to maintain personal ties and keep communications channels open. Those are the risks America faces right now. Amid extraordinary polarization and mistrust, it might not take much for things to spiral completely out of control and endanger social peace.

Take a Conservative or Liberal to Lunch

To overcome hyperconflict, several steps are needed to de-escalate societal tensions. Research has shown that if people have direct, personal experience with those who are different from themselves, they are more likely to form constructive relationships. Rather than seeing the other person as a member of an adversarial group, their personal interactions help them see past the identity to the individual him- or herself.[51]

This is one of the reasons why it is important to engage in a practice I call "take a conservative or liberal to lunch." Right now, America is dangerously divided by viewpoint, background, and lifestyle. It is hard for liberals and conservatives or Republicans and Democrats to understand one another's viewpoint. It is much easier to doubt opponents' perspectives and question their motives.

But if people talk with those having alternative viewpoints, it would help them see their adversaries as individuals, not dangerous adversaries. Having personal relationships across party or ideological lines would weaken polarization by putting a human face on the conflict. Rather than seeing opponents as enemies, they would come to view them as just having another point of view.

Yet there are other changes that need to take place beyond diversifying personal relationships. One of the issues that aggravates societal tensions is residential and educational sorting. People are separating themselves by where they live, how they are educated, and where they go for entertainment. This kind of behavior makes it hard to meet people who are different from oneself and gain an understanding of their backgrounds and experiences.

Another thing that contributes to people's separation is the nature of news coverage. Viewers have their own facts, and the news media have segmented into political niches that people rely on to reinforce their own prior beliefs. Most individuals do not seek information from a diverse range of sources but rather prefer confirmation of what they already believe. In this situation, it is important for consumers of news to broaden their news sources so they get a fairer sense of what is going on. Failure to do this will put America on a path toward even greater misunderstanding and distrust.

It is crucial to make sure technology does not further social divisions within the United States. Digital tools can facilitate extremism by making it easy for people to interact only with like-minded souls.

Developing new algorithms that bring people together and expose them to diverse information is vital.[52] Without a range of viewpoints, it will be hard to bring society together.

Accompanying this change in information gathering should come fundamental political reforms that discourage electoral extremism. Universal voting requirements could tame some of our current polarization. By raising turnout to the 90 percent levels seen in places that use this system, candidates would have few incentives to play to the base and emphasize extreme perspectives. American politics could move in a direction that is more moderate, civil, and respectful of political differences.[53]

The country furthermore needs to figure out ways to improve economic opportunity for all people. Right now, income inequality has risen dramatically over the past few decades, and this has intensified political conflict. Restoring the American Dream and improving education opportunity are vital for long-term conflict resolution. As Robert Putnam has pointed out, people need to feel they and their offspring have a fair shot at personal advancement.[54]

Reducing corruption and insider advantage is vital to restoring trust in government, business, and society. As long as people see the system as rigged against them, it will be hard to make progress. Those beliefs will fuel anger and resentment, and a sense that things are not equitable. Building an inclusive society that benefits a wide range of people is the best way to promote long-term security and prosperity.

Even with these steps forward, there are no guarantees that hyperconflict will subside anytime soon. High levels of societal tensions built over a long period of time will not easily recede. But that does not mean we should not try to reduce these divisions. Making progress in this area is vital for the future of the country and the world.

ACKNOWLEDGMENTS

This book draws on conversations with dozens of people over several decades. I use these discussions plus letters, notes, news articles, public opinion data, and social media posts to analyze how Americans have become so polarized and why liberals and conservatives have such negative views about each other. In reviewing activities over the past forty years, I recognize others may have perceptions that vary from mine or may draw different conclusions from mine. But I present my reminiscences and experiences based on my recollections of those events. All the individuals described in this book are real. There are no fictional or composite characters.

My parents, Robert and Jean West, my siblings, Shirley Mitchell, Joanne Shaver, and Ken West, my nieces, Laura Atkins, Katie Brewer, and Amy Leskoyak, my nephews Doug and Mark Mitchell and Jeff Shaver, and many aunts, uncles, and cousins shared many discussions about American politics that helped me better understand the views of conservatives and liberals and why there are disagreements over major political, economic, and religious issues.

Over the years, many people have contributed greatly to my life and my understanding of polarization. This includes my childhood friends Glen Blacker, Scott Chapin, Richard Charles, Marilyn Gibbons, Rosalind Murphy Jamieson, Tracy Keller, Linda Greene, Janice Baker Stewart, Dale Thomas, and Cheryl Toney and high school friends Karen Garrett Cutler, Cindy Davis, Cathy Hoppel Harrall, Linda Hoppel, Jeff Kissick, Larry Poos, Vic Snively, and Jake Taylor.

While in college at Miami University of Ohio, I was blessed with good friends and insightful academic advisers: Amy Bluestone Klein, Steven DeLue, David Golden, Laine Hawxhurst, Beth Germon Ignaut, Janet and Tom Larson, Vicky Markell Joseph, Jeanne Fischbach Laguilhemie, David McClellan, Paul Rejai, Phil Russo, Herb Waltzer, and Jim Woodworth.

During my graduate student days at Indiana University, a number of individuals helped refine my thinking: Christine Barbour, Ted Carmines, Alfred Diamant, Jeff Fishel, Linda Marianos Goetze, David Gopoian, Marjorie Hershey, Jim Kuklinski, Wayne Parent, Michael Pogue, Leroy Riselbach, David Robertson, David Webber, Ron Weber, and Judy Bryan Ziehm.

Over the twenty-six years I spent in Providence, Rhode Island, teaching at Brown University, numerous people pushed my perspective: Jeff Anderson, Peter Andreas, Tom Anton, Charlie Bakst, Mark and Janette Bertness, Buddy Cianci, David Cicilline, Emily Dietsch, Mary Fennell, Ed Fitzpatrick, Tara Granahan, Kathy Gregg, Betty-Jo Greene, Brian Hawkins, Dennis Hogan, Mary Housley, Jim Hummel, Patrick Kennedy, Dyana Koelsch, Baruch Korff, Janet Grace Krueger, Merle Krueger, Jim Langevin, Scott MacKay, Walter and Wanda McLaughlin, Jim Miller, Jim Morone, Marion Orr, Mark Patinkin, Marissa Quinn, Bill Rappleye, Jack Reed, Bob Reichley, Nancy Rosenblum, Wendy Schiller, Rebecca Spencer, Jim Taricani, Al Taubman, Gene Valicenti, Doug White, Happy White, Jack White, John Hazen White Jr., John Hazan White Sr., Sheldon Whitehouse, Patrice Wood, and Alan Zuckerman.

The past decade at the Brookings Institution in Washington, D.C., has been unusually eventful from the standpoint of American politics. I appreciate the contributions many individuals there have made to my personal and professional development: John Allen, Bill Antholis, Irena Barisic, Jacky Basile, Ashley Bennett, Steve Bennett, Jen Berlin, Bari Biern, Bob Brier, Brigitte Brown, Camille Busette, Michael Cavadel, Kim Churches, Leti Davalos, E. J. Dionne, Ona Dosunmu, Courtney Dunakin, Norm Eisen, Bill Gale, Bill Galston, Ted Gayer, Anna Goodbaum, Emily Horne, Christine Jacobs, Elaine Kamarck, Jenny Lu Mallamo, Tom Mann, Greg McGovern, Pietro Nivola, Emily Perkins, Liz Sablich, Hillary Schaub, Scott Sedar, Louis Serino, Strobe Talbott, Nicol Turner Lee, Liz Valentini, Tracy Viselli, Ben Wittes, Beth Stone Wood, and Niam Yaraghi.

I wish to thank several people for their help with this book. I am indebted to Karin Rosnizeck and Annie Schmitt for many helpful conversations about the book. This volume would not have been possible without their thoughtful suggestions. Jack Karsten and Hillary Schaub provided valuable research assistance on this project. A number of individuals at the Brookings Institution Press deserve a special thank-you. Press director William Finan and assistant director and sales manager Yelba Quinn provided invaluable counsel on the title and content of the book. Katherine Kimball did an outstanding job editing the manuscript. Elliott Beard designed and typeset the pages. Philip Pascuzzo came up with a creative cover design. None of these people are responsible for the interpretations, which are mine alone.

NOTES

Preface

1. "Palin, Paul, Trump: A GOP Convention Nightmare," *Arena* (blog), *Politico*, July 16, 2012.

2. Darrell M. West, *Billionaires: Reflections on the Upper Crust* (Brookings, 2014).

3. Darrell M. West, "U.S. Billionaires Political Power Index," Brookings Institution, 2014.

4. Michael Rothfeld and Joe Palazzolo, "Trump Lawyer Arranged $130,000 Payment for Adult-Film Star's Silence," *Wall Street Journal*, January 12, 2018; Jim Rutenberg, Megan Twohey, Rebecca Ruiz, Mike McIntire, and Maggie Haberman, "Tools of Trump's Fixer: Payouts, Intimidation, and the Tabloids," *New York Times*, February 18, 2018; William Rashbaum, Danny Hakim, Brian Rosenthal, Emily Flitter, and Jesse Drucker, "How Trump's Fixer Built Shadowy Business Empire," *New York Times*, May 6, 2018, p. A1.

5. Darrell M. West, "How I Upset Donald Trump and a Few Other Powerful Billionaires," *The Atlantic*, December 5, 2014.

6. Lilliana Mason, *Uncivil Agreement: How Politics Became Our Identity* (University of Chicago Press, 2018).

7. "West Family History," compiled by Shirley West Mitchell, 2008, Darrell

M. West Family History (www.InsidePolitics.org/DWestFamilyHistory.html), p. 68.

8. Ben Leubsdorf, "The Brown Daily Herald Poll," *Brown Daily Herald*, February 7, 2006.

9. Asawin Suebsaeng, "Trump Dined with Fox News' Seb Gorka and Jesse Watters at the White House This Week," *Daily Beast*, March 9, 2018.

10. Bill O'Reilly and Jesse Watters, "Brown U. Party Stirs Controversy," *The O'Reilly Factor*, Fox News Network, November 14, 2005. Also see Eric Beck, "Chaos and Management Failures Marred Sex Power God," *Brown Daily Herald*, April 27, 2006.

11. O'Reilly and Watters, "Brown U. Party Stirs Controversy."

12. Verne Gay, "What's Hate Got to Do with It?" *Newsday*, October 18, 2005.

13. Vic Snively, letter dated June 18, 2000, "Letters of a College Professor, 1992–2007," Darrell M. West Manuscripts (www.InsidePolitics.org/DWestPubs.html), p. 182.

14. Laura Mitchell, letter dated November 15, 1994, "Letters of a College Professor, 1992–2007," p. 41.

Chapter 1

1. Darrell M. West, *Making Campaigns Count* (Westport, Conn.: Greenwood Press, 1984).

2. James Stewart, *Blood Sport: The President and His Adversaries* (Simon & Schuster, 1997).

3. *Wikipedia*, s.v. "John Birch Society," February 12, 2006.

4. IMDb, *Dr. Strangelove or: How I Learned to Stop Worrying and Love the Bomb*, directed by Stanley Kubrick (Columbia Pictures, 1964).

5. Margot Hornblower, "Suicide and the Bomb Rouse Debate at Brown; Referendum on Cyanide Pills Unsettles Campus," *Washington Post*, October 10, 1984, p. A3.

6. Editorial, *Brown Daily Herald*, October 1984.

7. "Brown Students Vote," *Washington Post*, October 13, 1984, p. A4.

8. Ed Hardy, "Media Man," *Brown Alumni Monthly*, April 1994, pp. 20–23.

9. Joanne West Shaver, letter dated January 28, 1998, "Letters of a College Professor, 1992–2007," Darrell M. West Manuscripts (www.InsidePolitics.org/DWestPubs.html), p. 149.

10. Joanne West Shaver, letter dated March 25, 1998, "Letters of a College Professor, 1992–2007," p. 151.

11. Joanne West Shaver, letter dated September 12, 2001, "Letters of a College Professor, 1992–2007," p. 202.

12. Jean West, letter dated September 24, 2001, "Letters of a College Professor, 1992–2007," p. 203.

13. Darrell M. West, letter dated January 12, 2006, "Letters of a College Professor, 1992–2007," p. 540.

14. Darrell M. West, interview by Bill O'Reilly, *The O'Reilly Factor*, Fox News Network, August 18, 2005.

15. West, interview.

16. Stu Woo, "Clinton Stresses Need for More Women 'At the Table,'" *Brown Daily Herald*, April 10, 2006.

17. Alden Eagle and Shaun Joseph, "Two Protesters Who Disrupted Sen. Clinton's Speech Rebut Herald Criticism," *Brown Daily Herald*, April 19, 2006.

18. Scott MacKay, "Hillary Clinton Raises Her Profile in R.I.; Bill Visits Federal Hill," *Providence Journal*, April 9, 2006.

19. Darrell M. West, letter dated April 18, 2006, "Letters of a College Professor, 1992–2007," p. 604.

20. Anne Wootton, "Obama Dismisses Cynicism, Advocates Hope," *Brown Daily Herald*, October 13, 2006. Also see Elizabeth Gudrais and Karen Ziner, "A Democratic Star Shines in R.I.," *Providence Journal*, October 13, 2006, p. B1.

21. Darrell M. West, letter dated January 30, 2009, Letters from Washington, D.C., 2007–2018, collected unpublished letters, in author's possession, p. 104.

22. Joanne West Shaver, letter dated January 29, 2009, and Doug Mitchell, letter dated January 29, 2009, Letters from Washington, D.C., 2007–2018, p. 103.

23. Mahita Gajanan, "A History of Trump Being Trolled at the White House Correspondents' Dinner," *Time*, April 27, 2017.

24. "Preble County Election Results," WHIO-TV, aired November 8, 2016.

25. "District of Columbia Results," *New York Times*, November 8, 2016.

26. Taneil Ruffin, "Clinton Receives 85 Percent of Student Support to Trump's 1.8," *Brown Daily Herald*, October 17, 2016.

27. Matthew Richardson, "Why I'm Still an Evangelical in the Age of Trump," *Financial Times*, October 25, 2018.

28. Jonathan Rauch and Benjamin Wittes, "Boycott the GOP," *The Atlantic*, March 2018, pp. 13– 16.

29. Anne Gearan and John Wagner, "Trump Calls Democratic Lawmakers Who Didn't Applaud Him 'Treasonous,' 'un-American,'" *Washington Post*, February 5, 2018.

30. Ken West, Facebook post, February 14, 2018.

31. Bob Snively, Facebook post, February 15, 2018.

32. Carolyn Portwood, Facebook post, February 16, 2018.

33. Matt Flegenheimer, "The Staying Power of a Salacious Story," *New York Times*, March 10, 2018, p. A15.

34. Author's notes based on Bette Midler, Twitter tweet, dated August 4, 2018.

35. Darrell M. West, Facebook page, January 30– 31, 2018.

Chapter 2

1. Jay Shambaugh and Ryan Nunn, "Why Wages Aren't Growing in America," *Harvard Business Review*, October 24, 2017.

2. Linda Greene, Facebook post, October 27, 2018.

3. Frank Howell, Yuk-Ying Tung, and Cynthia Wade-Harper, "The Social Cost of Growing Up in Rural America," Mississippi State University, October 1996.

4. The 1800 and 1850 numbers come from "Agriculture," *Digital History*, January 23, 2018 (www.digitalhistory.uh.edu/disp_textbook.cfm?smtID= 11&psid=3837), while the 1900 and 1950 percentages are based on "Farmers & the Land," *Growing a Nation*, January 23, 2018 (www.agclassroom.org/ gan/timeline/farmers_land.htm); the 2000 number is based on U.S. Federal Reserve of St. Louis, "Percent of Employment in Agriculture in the United States," January 23, 2018. Also see Patricia Daly, "Agricultural Employment: Has the Decline Ended?" *Monthly Labor Review*, November 1981.

5. Ken West, personal letter to author, dated July 25, 2018.

6. Thomas Frank, *What's the Matter with Kansas?* (New York: Henry Holt, 2004).

7. Bret Wallach, *A World Made for Money* (University of Nebraska Press, 2015), p. 210. Also see Karl Plume, "U.S. Dairy Farms in Crisis as Milk Prices Turn Sour," Reuters, February 9, 2009.

8. Mark Patinkin, "What I Learned from Making Hay in the Summer," *Providence Journal*, June 17, 2003, p. G1.

9. Boris Simkovich, "Long-Term Trends in American Intergenerational Occupational Mobility," Harvard University, undated paper, in author's possession.

10. J. D. Vance, *Hillbilly Elegy: A Memoir of a Family and Culture in Crisis* (New York: Harper, 2016).

11. U.S. Federal Reserve of St. Louis, "Percent of Employment in Manufacturing in the United States," January 19, 2018.

12. Vic Snively, letter dated October 1, 1982, "Letters of a College Student, 1974–1983," Darrell M. West Manuscripts (www.InsidePolitics.org/DWest Pubs.html), p. 290.

13. Vic Snively, letter dated January 4, 2006, "Letters of a College Professor, 1992–2007," Darrell M. West Manuscripts (www.InsidePolitics.org/DWest Pubs.html), p. 539.

14. Tracy Keller, letter dated December 13, 2006, "Letters of a College Professor, 1992–2007," p. 768.

15. Katharine Seelye, "One Son, Six Hours, Four Overdoses: A Family's Anguish," *New York Times*, January 21, 2018, p. A1.

16. Joanne West Shaver, letter dated February 7, 1996, "Letters of a College Professor, 1992–2007," p. 76.

17. Joanne West Shaver, letter dated December 10, 1996, "Letters of a College Professor, 1992–2007," p. 122.

18. Joanne West Shaver, letter dated April 20, 1993, "Letters of a College Professor, 1992–2007," p. 18.

19. Lawrence Mishel, Elise Gould, and Josh Bivens, "Stagnant Wages for Middle-Wage Workers, Declining Wages for Low-Wage Workers," Economic Policy Institute, January 6, 2015.

20. Jay Shambaugh and Ryan Nunn, "Why Wages Aren't Growing in America," *Harvard Business Review*, October 24, 2017.

21. Thomas Piketty and Emmanuel Saez, "Income Inequality in the United States, 1913–1998," *Quarterly Journal of Economics* 118 (2003), pp. 1–39. For 1999 to 2012 numbers, see "Tables and Figures Updated to 2017" at the web page of Emmanuel Saez (http://emlab.berkeley.edu/users/saez).

22. Darrell M. West, letter dated March 1, 2009, Letters from Washington, D.C., 2007–2018, collected unpublished letters, in author's possession, p. 107.

Chapter 3

1. Richard Reeves, "Planning the American Dream: The Case for an Office of Opportunity," Brookings Institution, Center on Children and Families, May, 2014, p. 3.

2. Robert Putnam, *Our Kids: The American Dream in Crisis* (Simon and Schuster, 2016), p. 2.

3. Jeannette Hays, "A History of Fairhaven," unpublished paper, 1961, in author's possession; and H. Z. Williams and Brothers, *History of Preble County, Ohio* (H. Z. Williams Publishing, 1881).

4. "What Family Travel Cost in 1954," *Deseret News*, July 8, 2008.

5. "Jean West Life Story," July 28, 2001, Darrell M. West Family History (www.InsidePolitics.org/DWestFamilyHistory.html).

6. "Jean West Life Story," July 28, 2001.

7. "Jean West Life Story." July 28, 2001.

8. Stacy Torian, "Breaking Through the Class Ceiling," *In the Fray*, March 6, 2005.

9. Robert Hauser and David Featherman, "Equality of Schooling: Trends and Prospects," *Sociology of Education* 49, no. 2, p. 99.

10. James Coleman, *Equality of Opportunity* (Washington: National Center for Education Statistics, 1966).

11. Peter English, *Rheumatic Fever in America and Britain* (East Brunswick, N.J.: Rutgers University Press, 1999).

12. "Deaths per 100,000 from Rheumatic Fever and Scarlet Fever, 1900–1960," *Vital Statistics of the United States*, UCLA Department of Economics, unpublished and undated paper.

13. Denise Grady, "Where a Sore Throat Becomes a Slow Death Sentence," *New York Times*, September 16, 2018, p. 1.

14. Laine Hawxhurst, letter dated October 2, 1974, "Letters of a College Student, 1974–1983," Darrell M. West Manuscripts (www.InsidePolitics.org/DWestPubs.html), p. 12.

15. Thomas Piketty and Emmanuel Saez, "Income Inequality in the United States, 1913–1998," *Quarterly Journal of Economics* 118 (2003), pp. 1–39. For 1999 to 2008 numbers, see the web page of Emmanuel Saez (http://emlab.berkeley.edu/users/saez). Also see Richard Burkhauser, Shuaiz Hang Feng, Stephen Jenkins, and Jeff Larrimore, "Recent Trends in Top Income Shares in the USA: Reconciling Estimates from March CPS and IRS Tax Return Data," Working Paper (Cambridge, Mass.: National Bureau of Economic Research,

September 2009). Also see Thomas Piketty, *Capital in the Twenty-First Century* (Cambridge, Mass.: Harvard University Press, 2014).

16. The 2012 income numbers come from Emmanuel Saez, "Striking It Richer: The Evolution of Top Incomes in the United States," unpublished paper, University of California, Berkeley, Department of Economics, September 3, 2013.

17. Anne Case and Angus Deaton, "Mortality and Morbidity in the Twenty-First Century," Brookings Panel on Economic Activity, May 1, 2017.

18. Eleanor Krause and Richard Reeves, "Rural Dreams: Upward Mobility in America's Countryside," Brookings Institution, Center on Children and Families, September 2017, p. 2.

19. Robert Putnam, *Our Kids: The American Dream in Crisis* (Simon &Schuster, 2016).

20. U.S. Department of Education, "Tuition Costs of Colleges and Universities," National Center for Education Statistics, Washington, D.C., 2016.

21. Peter Coy, "A Tenured Professor Says Most of What We Learn in College, and Even High School, Is Useless," *Bloomberg Businessweek*, January 22, 2018, p. 13.

22. Stef Kight and Harry Stevens, "Being 30, Then and Now," *Axios*, July 23, 2018.

23. Quoted in Richard Reeves and Katherine Guyot, "Fewer Americans Are Making More Than Their Parents Did—Especially If They Grew Up in the Middle Class," *Up Front* (blog), Brookings Institution, July 25, 2018.

Chapter 4

1. Amy Chua, *Political Tribes: Group Instinct and the Fate of Nations* (New York: Penguin Press, 2018). Also see Jonathan Rauch, "Have Our Tribes Become More Important Than Our Country?," *Washington Post*, February 16, 2018.

2. George Eberstadt, "Ring In the New Year by Dialing Down the Negativity," *Turn to Networks*, December 29, 2017.

3. Eberstadt, "Ring In the New Year."

4. Ruth Logue, "Memories of Hazel Laverne Crist West," unpublished and undated paper, in author's possession.

5. Ruth Logue, "Memories of Walter Lawrence West," unpublished and undated paper, in author's possession.

6. "West Maternal Family Genealogy, 1814–1980," Darrell M. West Family History (www.InsidePolitics.org/DWestFamilyHistory.html).

7. Emma Steele, letter to Martha Steele, November 15, 1925, "Steele Family Letters, 1916–1933," Darrell M. West Family History, pp. 18–19 (www.InsidePolitics.org/DWestFamilyHistory.html).

8. Dorothy Steele diary, 1961, in author's possession.

9. "Jean West Life Story," July 28, 2001, Darrell M. West Family History (www.InsidePolitics.org/DWestFamilyHistory.html).

10. Kenneth West, "My Life Story in My Own Words," Autumn 2014, p. 148, unpublished paper, in author's possession.

11. Darrell M. West, letter dated July 25, 2010, Letters from Washington, D.C., 2007–2018, collected unpublished letters, in author's possession, p. 159.

12. "'Rape List' on Bathroom Walls Spurs Furor at Brown University," *St. Louis Post-Dispatch*, December 16, 1990, p. 9D; William Celis, "Date Rape and a List at Brown," *New York Times*, November 18, 1990.

13. Bari Weiss, "What Do You Do When You Are Anonymously Accused of Rape?" *New York Times*, October 13, 2018.

14. "'Rape List' on Bathroom Walls Spurs Furor at Brown University."

15. "'Rape List' on Bathroom Walls Spurs Furor at Brown University."

16. Morgan McVicar, "Brown's Handling of Sexual Assault Complaint Splits Campus," *Providence Journal*, December 15, 1996, p. A1; Morgan McVicar, "Students Settle Suit with Brown, Accuser," *Providence Journal*, January 1, 1998.

17. McVicar, "Brown's Handling of Sexual Assault Complaint Splits Campus."

18. "Adam Michael Lack: A Dead Zone Death," Iowa Cold Cases (IowaColdCases.org), October 15, 2016 (https://iowacoldcases.org/case-summaries/adam-lack/).

19. McVicar, "Brown's Handling of Sexual Assault Complaint Splits Campus."

20. McVicar, "Brown's Handling of Sexual Assault Complaint Splits Campus."

21. Morgan McVicar, "20/20 Vision? Tempest over Sexual Assault Outdoor Rally at Brown Degenerates into Rhetorical Melee with TV Reporter," *Providence Journal*, January 30, 1997, p. B1.

22. McVicar, "20/20 Vision? Tempest over Sexual Assault."

23. Chaz Firestone, "Times Columnist Pied in Face by Activist," *Brown Daily Herald*, April 23, 2008.

24. Carla Blumenkranz, "Meaning of Campus Protest in Question," *Brown Daily Herald*, April 10, 2003.

25. Marion Davis, "Anger at Brown Still Simmers over Divisive Ad," *Providence Journal*, April 8, 2001, p. A1; Linda Borg, "Ad Sparks Angry Protest at Brown," *Providence Journal*, March 17, 2001, p. A3.

26. David Estlund, "Stealing Newspapers for Free Speech," *Providence Journal*, April 6, 2001, p. B5.

27. Linda Borg, "Brown Closes Speech Forum," *Providence Journal*, March 22, 2001, p. A1; Linda Borg, "Brown Administrators Defend Barring Public from Forum," *Providence Journal*, March 23, 2001.

28. Paul Davis, "Report Details Brown's, State's Slave-Trading Roots," *Providence Journal*, October 19, 2006, p. A1.

29. Belluck, "Brown U. to Examine Debt to Slave Trade."

30. Dana Goldstein, "Slavery and Justice Committee Brings National Media to Brown," *Brown Daily Herald*, March 22, 2004; Belluck, "Brown U. to Examine Debt to Slave Trade."

31. Pam Belluck, "Panel Suggests Brown U. Atone for Ties to Slavery," *New York Times*, October 19, 2006

32. Sara Molinaro, "RUF Back on Campus," *Brown Daily Herald*, February 6, 2007.

33. Laura Ingraham, "Evangelical Group Suspended from Campus," *The O'Reilly Factor*, Fox News Network, November 20, 2006.

34. Scott MacKay, "Brown Offers Reinstatement to Religious Group," *Providence Journal*, November 28, 2006, p. B1; Molinaro, "RUF Back on Campus."

35. Thomas Morgan, "Protesters Boo NYC Police Commissioner Kelly from Stage at Brown University," *Providence Journal*, October 29, 2013.

36. Morgan, "Protesters Boo NYC Police Commissioner Kelly."

37. Maxine Joselow and Jillian Lanney, "Kelly Lecture Spurs Student, Community Backlash," *Brown Daily Herald*, October 29, 2013.

38. David Carr and Tim Arango, "A Fox Chief at the Pinnacle of Media and Politics," *New York Times*, January 9, 2010.

39. Maureen Dowd, "'Riling Up the Crazies,'" *New York Times*, October 28, 2018.

40. Darrell M. West, letter dated November 19, 2010, Letters from Washington, D.C., 2007–2018, p. 166.

41. Roger Ailes, letter dated November 24, 2010, Letters from Washington, D.C., 2007–2018, p. 167.

42. Darrell M. West, "Trump's Executive Order on Unions Will Hurt Federal Employees," *FixGov* (blog), Brookings Institution, May 29, 2018.

43. U.S. House Government Operations Subcommittee hearing, "Union Time on the People's Dime: A Closer Look at Official Time," YouTube, May 24, 2018.

44. Mary Troyan, "Ethics Probe of Rep. Mark Meadows Continues," *USA Today*, August 17, 2016; Sam Stein, "Ex–Mark Meadows Aide Says Sexual Harassment in Congressman's Office Was Known Earlier Than Reported," *Daily Beast*, January 16, 2018.

45. U.S. House Government Operations Subcommittee Hearing, "Union Time on the People's Dime," May 24, 2018 (https://oversight.house.gov/hearing/union-time-on-the-peoples-dime-a-closer-look-at-official-time/).

46.Todd Graham, "An 'Oops' That Could Mean 'Over' for Perry," *CNN*, November 10, 2011.

47. Maeve Reston, "'I Will Never Forget': Christine Blasey Ford Recounts Her Trauma in Raw Testimony," *CNN*, September 27, 2018.

48. Sheryl Stolberg and Nicholas Fandos, "Brett Kavanaugh and Christine Blasey Ford Duel with Tears and Fury," *New York Times*, September 27, 2018.

49. Jennifer Agiesta, "Majority Oppose Kavanaugh, but His Popularity Grows with GOP," *CNN*, October 8, 2018.

50. Yochai Benkler, Robert Faris, and Hal Roberts, *Network Propaganda: Manipulation, Disinformation, and Radicalization in American Politics* (New York: Oxford University Press, 2018).

Chapter 5

1. James Morone, *Hellfire Nation: The Politics of Sin in American History* (Yale University Press, 2004).

2. Tara Westover, *Educated: A Memoir* (New York: Random House, 2018).

3. Ruth Logue, "Memories of Lawrence Philander West," unpublished and undated paper, in author's possession.

4. Kenneth West, "My Life Story in My Own Words," Autumn 2014, unpublished paper, in author's possession, p. 147.

5. Deborah Mullen, "What It Means to Be Black and Christian in the 21st Century," McCormick Theological Seminary, undated, unpublished paper, in author's possession,.

6. Allison Wentz, "Social Activist Angela Davis Packs Salomon," *Brown Daily Herald*, February 8, 2008.

7. Gnostic Society Library, "The Nag Hammadi Library," undated (http://gnosis.org/naghamm/nhl.html).

8. CenturyOne Bookstore, "Dead Sea Scrolls," undated (www.centuryone.com/25dssfacts.html).

9. Bart Ehrman, *Misquoting Jesus: The Story behind Who Changed the Bible and Why* (Harper San Francisco, 2005).

10. Elaine Pagels, *Beyond Belief: The Secret Gospel of Thomas* (New York: Random House, 2003).

11. Ehrman, *Misquoting Jesus*.

12. Shirley West Mitchell, letter dated September 30, 1981, "Letters of a College Student, 1974–1983," Darrell M. West Manuscripts (www.Inside Politics.org/DWestPubs.html), p. 278.

13. Joanne West Shaver, letter dated September 7, 1978, "Letters of a College Student, 1974–1983," p. 229.

14. Darrell M. West, letter dated February 6, 1977, "Letters of a College Student, 1974–1983," p. 141.

15. Deborah Caldwell, "The Christianity Battles," *Belief Net*, 2006, in the author's possession.

16. Darrell M. West, "Travel Journals: Israel, 2007," Darrell M. West Travel Journals (www.InsidePolitics.org/DWestPubs.html).

17. Christine Rosen, *My Fundamentalist Education: A Memoir of a Divine Girlhood* (New York: Public Affairs, 2006).

18. Doane Hulick, "Hightower Sues State over the Outcome of His Trial for Murder," *Providence Journal*, March 3, 1994, p. D11.

19. D. James Kennedy, statement to Reclaiming America for Christ conference, February 2005, quoted in Wikiquote, s.v. "James Kennedy." See also "The Rise of the Religious Right in the Republican Party," February 2011 (http://theocracywatch.org/#how)

20. "America's Changing Religious Landscape," Pew Research Center, May 12, 2015.

21. Joanne West Shaver, letter dated May 9, 1995, "Letters of a College Professor, 1992–2007," Darrell M. West Manuscripts (www.InsidePolitics.org/DWestPubs.html), p. 58.

22. Darrell M. West, letter dated January 12, 2006, "Letters of a College Professor, 1992–2007," p. 540.

23. Mark Mitchell, letter dated August 22, 1999, "Letters of a College Professor, 1992–2007," pp. 169–170.

24. Daniel Bergner, "The Call," *New York Times Magazine,* January 29, 2006, pp. 40–46, 72–75.

25. Joanne West Shaver, letter dated April 4, 1997, "Letters of a College Professor, 1992–2007," p. 130.

26. Shirley West Mitchell, letter dated February 17, 2016, Letters from Washington, D.C., 2007–2018, collected unpublished letters, in author's possession, p. 258.

27. Joanne West Shaver, letter dated August 5, 2004, "Letters of a College Professor, 1992–2007," p. 407.

28. "Bob West Life Story," 1985, Darrell M. West Family History (www. InsidePolitics.org/DWestFamilyHistory.html).

29. Noah Feldman, "Divided by God: Religion and Government in America," lecture delivered at Central Congregational Church, Providence, Rhode Island, January 26, 2018.

30. Kelsey Dallas, "How Justice Scalia Ruled on Religious Freedom—and Why It Matters," *Deseret News,* February 25, 2016.

31. Josh Gerstein, "SCOTUS Makes Narrow Ruling on Same-Sex Wedding," *Politico,* June 5, 2018, p. 7.

32. Joanne West Shaver, conversation with the author, June 5, 2018.

33. Sharon Nordmeyer Hope, Facebook post, June 20, 2018.

34. Gayle Myrick, "You Can't Make State Officials Like Me Perform Same-Sex Marriages," *Washington Post,* February 14, 2018.

35. Cited by Ken West from Meria Heller, "Best Meme of the Day," August 29, 2018.

Chapter 6

1. Darrell M. West, *Brain Gain: Rethinking U.S. Immigration Policy* (Brookings, 2010).

2. Darrell M. West, "Travel Journals: Lebanon, 2002," Darrell M. West Travel Journals (www.InsidePolitics.org/DWestPubs.html).

3. West, "Travel Journals: Lebanon, 2002."

4. Darrell M. West, "Travel Journals: Bahrain, 2005," Darrell M. West Travel Journals (www.InsidePolitics.org/DWestPubs.html).

5. Portions of this are taken from Darrell M. West, "Inside the Immigration Process," Brookings Institution Op-Ed, April 15, 2013.

6. Vartan Gregorian, letter dated May 20, 2013, Letters from Washington,

D.C., 2007–2018, collected unpublished letters, in author's possession, p. 226.

7. Linda Greene, letter dated October 13, 2016, Letters from Washington, D.C., 2007–2018, pp. 273–74.

8. Declan Walsh, "As Strongmen Steamroll Their Opponents, Trump Is Silent," *New York Times*, February 1, 2018.

9. Andrew James Gregor, Twitter tweet, June 10, 2018.

10. Stephen O'Rourke, Facebook post, June 15, 2018.

11. Sarah Carr, "Tomorrow's Test," *Slate*, June 5, 2016.

12. Dudley Poston and Rogelio Saenz, "U.S. Whites Will Soon Be the Minority in Number, but Not Power," *Baltimore Sun*, August 8, 2017.

13. William Frey, "The US Will Become 'Minority White' in 2045, Census Projects," "The Avenue," Brookings Institution blog, Michael Walsh, "US Percentage of Non-Hispanic Whites Hits All-Time Low of 63%," *New York Daily News*, June 13, 2013; Sandra Colby and Jennifer Ortman, "Projections of the Size and Composition of the US Population: 2014–2060," Bureau of the Census, March 3, 2015.

14. William Galston, "Is Increasing Diversity Positive for the U.S.? A Look at the Partisan Divide," *FixGov* (blog), Brookings, July 19, 2018.

15. Emily Swanson and Russell Contreras, "Most Americans Say Trump Is Racist," *Associated Press*, March 1, 2018.

16. Steve Phillips, "Trump Wants to Make America White Again," *New York Times*, February 15, 2018.

17. Shirley West Mitchell, e-mail, October 13, 2018.

Chapter 7

1. Elmer Cornwell and Jay Goodman, *The Politics of the Rhode Island Constitutional Convention* (Washington, D.C.: National Municipal League, 1969).

2. Christopher Rowland, "The DiPrete Case: Officials and Politicians Stunned, Saddened by Pleas," *Providence Journal*, December 12, 1998, p. A14.

3. Mike Stanton, "Cianci Indicted," *Providence Journal*, April 3, 2001.

4. Mike Stanton, *The Prince of Providence* (Random House, 2003).

5. Darrell M. West, *Billionaires: Reflections on the Upper Crust* (Brookings, 2014).

6. Rachael Bade, "Rand Paul in Cross Hairs of Tax Evasion War," *Politico*, March 2, 2014.

7. Michael Schmidt, Eric Lipton, and Alexandra Stevenson, "After Big

Bet, Hedge Fund Pulls the Levers of Power," *New York Times*, March 9, 2014.

8. Fox Butterfield, "Brown Outpacing Rivals in Ivy League Popularity," *New York Times*, March 20, 1983.

9. Darrell M. West, *Patrick Kennedy: The Rise to Power* (Upper Saddle River, N.J.: Prentice-Hall, 2000), p. 160.

10. Daniel Golden, *The Price of Admission: How America's Ruling Class Buys Its Way into Elite Colleges—and Who Gets Left Outside the Gates* (New York: Broadway Books, 2007).

11. Nicholas Kristof, "Liberal Hypocrisy in College Admissions?" *New York Times*, October 28, 2018.

12. Anemona Hartocollis, Amy Harmon, and Mitch Smith, "'Lopping,' 'Tips,' and the 'Z-List': Bias Lawsuit Explores Harvard's Admissions Secrets," *New York Times*, July 29, 2018.

13. Anemona Hartocollis, "A Peek Behind the Ivy: How to Get Into Harvard," *New York Times*, October 20, 2018, p. 1.

14. Darrell M. West, letter dated October 27, 2004, "Letters of a College Professor, 1992–2007," Darrell M. West Manuscripts (www.InsidePolitics.org/DWestPubs.html), p. 439.

15. Melanie Wolfgang, "Hoffman Tells Actors to Expect—and Embrace—Failure," *Brown Daily Herald*, October 25, 2004.

16. Eric Lipton and Brooke Williams, "How Think Tanks Amplify Corporate America's Influence," *New York Times*, August 7, 2016, p. 1.

17. Emily Tamkin, "Washington Think Tanks Still Divided on Whether to Return Saudi Donations over Journalist's Disappearance," *BuzzFeed News*, October 17, 2018.

Chapter 8

1. Julia Azari, "Politics Is More Partisan Now, but It's Not More Divisive," *FiveThirtyEight.com*, January 19, 2018.

2. Adam Bonica, Nolan McCarty, Keith T. Poole, and Howard Rosenthal. 2015, "Congressional Polarization and Its Connection to Income Inequality," *American Gridlock: The Sources, Character, and Impact of Congressional Polarization*, pp. 357–77, edited by James A. Thurber and Antoine Yoshinaka (New York: Cambridge University Press, 2015).

3. Hannah Fingerhut, "Why Do People Belong to a Party? Negative Views of the Opposing Party Are a Major Factor," unpublished paper, Pew Research Center, March 29, 2018.

4. Jaime Settle, *Frenemies: How Social Media Polarizes America* (Cambridge University Press, 2018).

5. Carolyn Portwood, Facebook post, May 30, 2018.

6. Bill and Pat Roberts, Facebook post, May 30, 2018.

7. Shibley Telhami and Stella Rouse, "America First? American National Identity Declines over Last Two Years among Both Republicans and Democrats," University of Maryland Critical Issues Poll, November, 2017.

8. Telhami and Rouse, "America First?"

9. Mark Leibovich, *Big Game: The NFL in Dangerous Times* (New York: Penguin Press, 2018), p. 227.

10. Bill Reynolds, "Like It or Not, Colin Kaepernick Follows His Heart," *Providence Journal*, September 22, 2018.

11. Hannah Fingerhut , "Republicans Much 'Colder' Than Democrats in Views of Professors," unpublished paper, Pew Research Center, September 13, 2017.

12. University of Michigan, "Trust the Federal Government," *ANES Guide to Public Opinion and Electoral Behavior, 1958–2012* (www.electionstudies.org/nesguide/toptable/tab5a_1.htm).

13. Seymour Martin Lipset and William Schneider, *The Confidence Gap* (New York: Free Press, 1983).

14. Daniel Drezner, "Edelman Surveyed Americans about Trust. The Findings Are Disturbing, but Not in the Way You Might Think," *Washington Post*, January 23, 2018.

15. "Trust in Government: 1958–2015," unpublished paper, Pew Research Center, November 23, 2015.

16. Ben Sasse, *Them: Why We Hate Each Other—and How to Heal* (New York: St. Martin's Press, 2018).

17. Lilliana Mason, *Uncivil Agreement: How Politics Became Our Identity* (University of Chicago Press, 2018), p. 45.

18. Steven Levitsky and Daniel Ziblatt, "How Wobbly Is Our Democracy?," *New York Times*, January 27, 2018.

19. Recounted in Joanne West Shaver, letter dated February 2, 2013, Letters from Washington, D.C., 2007–2018, collected unpublished letters, in author's possession, p. 213.

20. Linda Greene, letter dated November 15, 2016, Letters from Washington, D.C., 2007–2018, p. 278.

21. Elizabeth Dias, "The Evangelical Fight to Win Back California," *New York Times*, May 27, 2018.

22. Joe Gilgan, Facebook post, July 26, 2018.

23. Harriet Sherwood, "The Chosen One? The New Film That Claims Trump's Election Was an Act of God," *The Guardian*, October 3, 2018.

24. Alan Abramowitz, *The Great Alignment: Race, Party Transformation, and the Rise of Donald Trump* (Yale University Press, 2018).

25. Amy Chua, *Political Tribes: Group Instinct and the Fate of Nations* (New York: Penguin Press, 2018).

26. Dave Barry, "An Off-Color Rift," *Washington Post*, December 19, 2004.

27. Darrell M. West, *Megachange: Economic Disruption, Political Upheaval, and Social Strife in the 21st Century* (Brookings, 2016).

28. Mason, *Uncivil Agreement*, pp. 128–29.

29. David Brooks, "Integration Now and Forever," *New York Times*, March 30, 2018, p. A21.

30. Eric Forbush and Nicol Turner Lee, "Can Social Media Help Build Communities?," paper presented at the Telecommunications Policy Research Conference, Washington, D.C., September 21–22, 2018.

31. Peter Schroeder, "Poll: 43 Percent of Republicans Believe Obama Is a Muslim," *The Hill*, September 13, 2015.

32. Jennifer Kavanagh and Michael Rich, *Truth Decay: An Initial Exploration of the Diminishing Role of Facts and Analysis in American Public Life* (Santa Monica, Calif.: RAND, 2018).

33. Annie Lowrey, "Left Economy, Right Economy," *The Atlantic*, June 4, 2018.

34. Quoted in Mike Allen, "Thought of the Day," *Axios AM*, May 24, 2018.

35. Aaron Hanlon, "Postmodernism Didn't Cause Trump. It Explains Him," *Washington Post*, August 31, 2018.

36. Tom Toles, "Everybody Is Now Entitled to Their Own Facts," *Washington Post*, September 10, 2015.

37. Ken West, phone call with author, March 3, 2018.

38. Darrell M. West, letter dated December 31, 2010, Letters from Washington, D.C., p. 174.

39. Miriam Weaver, "There Has Never Been a Better Description of Trump in the History of Ever," *Chicks on the Right*, October 23, 2018.

40. William Cummings, "Iowa Rep. Steve King Says America Is Heading toward Another Civil War," *USA Today*, June 25, 2018.

41. Eli Rosenberg, "Six Siblings Say Don't Vote for Their Brother, an Arizona Congressman," *Providence Journal*, September 22, 2018.

42. "Another Political Family Feud Emerges, This Time in the Nevada Governor's Race," *CNN Politics*, September 30, 2018.

43. Matt Viser and Robert Costa, "'An Angry Mob': Republicans Work to Recast Democratic Protests as Out-Of-Control Anarchy," *Washington Post*, October 8, 2018.

44. Chris Foreman, Facebook post, October 20, 2018.

45. Viser and Costa, "'An Angry Mob.'"

46. Jordain Carney, "Rand Paul on Political Climate," *The Hill*, October 9, 2018.

47. William Rashbaum, "Pipe Bombs Sent to Hillary Clinton, Barack Obama and CNN Offices," *New York Times*, October 24, 2018.

48. Mike Allen, "Political Terrorism in America," *Axios PM*, October 24, 2018. Also see Marvin Kalb, *Enemy of the People: Trump's War on the Press, the New McCarthyism, and the Threat to American Democracy* (Brookings Institution Press, 2018).

49. Lauri Goodstein, "'There Is Still So Much Evil': Growing Anti-Semitism Stuns American Jews," *New York Times*, October 29, 2018.

50. Emma Steele, letter to Martha Steele, July 24, 1932, "Steele Family Letters, 1916–1933," Darrell M. West Family History (www.InsidePolitics.org/DWestFamilyHistory.html), p. 30.

51. Jennifer Hochschild, "American Racial and Ethnic Politics in the 21st Century," Brookings Institution report, March 1, 1998; Robin DeAngelo, "Why It's So Hard to Talk to White People about Racism," *Huffington Post*, April 30, 2015.

52. Darrell M. West, *The Future of Work: Robots, AI, and Automation* (Brookings, 2018).

53. William Galston and E. J. Dionne, "The Case for Universal Voting: Why Making Voting a Duty Would Enhance Our Elections and Improve Our Government," Center for Effective Public Management, Brookings Institution, September 2015, p. 4.

54. Robert Putnam, *Our Kids: The American Dream in Crisis* (Simon & Schuster, 2016).

INDEX

Abortion, 3, 41, 75, 103, 109

Abramowitz, Alan, 176

Abuse: of children, 46, 48; domestic, 46, 158; substance abuse, 45–47, 66, 101. *See also* Sexual harassment

Academics. *See* Education

Ackman, William, 150

Admissions process, 151–55

Affirmative action, 6, 86, 154

Affordable Care Act (2010), 30, 37, 67, 123–24

Agriculture, 40–45; communist systems of, 108; dairy farms, 10–11, 41–43, 145–46; embargoes and tariffs related to, 40–41; hay baling, 43–44; immigrant labor in, 128–29, 141; percentage of workforce in, 40; planting and harvesting, 43, 54; profit sharing in, 54–55; rural areas impacted by decline of, 41, 45; self-sustainability through, 57

Ailes, Roger, 92–94

Alcohol abuse. *See* Substance abuse

Allen, John, 165

Aluminum tariffs, 40

American Dream, 54, 65, 67–68, 187

Anthem demonstrations, 171

Anti-Semitism, 184

Anton, Tom, 161, 162

Assault, sexual, 80–85, 100

Atheism, 74, 108, 109

Atkins, Doug, 30, 119, 121

Atkins, Laura, 8, 118, 119

Authoritarianism, 33, 35, 140, 165, 180

Azari, Julia, 167

Family-based tribalism, 70–72

Farming. *See* Agriculture

Featherman, David, 57

Females. *See* Women

Fluoridation of water, 13

Food embargo (1973), 40

Forbush, Eric, 177–78

Fox News, 6, 26, 90, 92–94, 101–02, 183

Freedom of speech, 87–88

Freedom of the press, 85, 87–88, 140

Friedman, Tom, 85–86

Fundamentalism, 104–10; biblical interpretations in, 104–05, 109, 113–14; communism as viewed in, 108–09; community-based churches in, 110; dilemma regarding doctrinal purity in, 115–16; growth of, 3; and political activism, 109–10, 118; revival meetings, 105–06; on salvation and redemption, 105–07; student organizations, 90–91; value of human soul in, 121

Fundraising practices, 89, 90, 159–65

Galston, William, 143

Gates, Bill, 2, 164

Gays. *See* Homosexuality

Gender-based tribalism, 79–85

"Get a senator" strategy, 149–50

Gingrich, Newt, 19, 22

Globalization, 127–31, 138, 143, 167

Golden, Daniel, 154

Goodman, Jay, 146

Gore, Al, 21–22

Gosar, Paul, 182–83

Grady, Don, 75

Graham, Franklin, 175

Grain embargo (1980), 40

Great Recession (2008–09), 30, 138, 172

Gregorian, Vartan, 138, 162–64

Gun control, 17, 30, 33

Gutowski, Ralph, 3–4

Haley, Harold, 107

Hand, Learned, 117

Harassment. *See* Sexual harassment

Harris, Kamala, 184

Harvard University, 5, 154–55, 160

Hauser, Robert, 57

Hay baling, 43–44

Health care: cost escalation for, 65; insurance for, 67; religious exemptions related to, 123–24; in rural areas, 56, 58–59; for uninsured, 17–18. *See also* Affordable Care Act

Hellfire Nation: The Politics of Sin in American History (Morone), 103

Herbalife, 150

Hightower, Christopher, 116–17

Hobby Lobby, 123–24

Hoffman, Dustin, 155–56

Holder, Eric, 184

Holmes, John, 147

Home ownership, 67

Homosexuality: biblical views of, 3–4, 78, 79; coming out process, 76–77; same-sex marriage, 3, 78–79, 103, 124, 125

Horowitz, David, 86, 87

Hyperconflict, 167–87; consequences of, 167–68, 176, 180; de-escalation strategies, 185–87; factors in